Early Church History

An Introduction

From the *Acts of the Apostles* to the fall of the Western Roman Empire

Lord of History Series
Volume I

ROBERT M. HADDAD

Early Church History

Dedication

In honor
of those who acknowledge
Jesus Christ
as Lord of History

*"It was his loving design, centered in Christ,
to give history its fulfilment by resuming everything in him,
all that is in heaven, all that is on earth,
summed up in him."*
(Eph. 1:9-10)

Foreword

The fathers of the Second Vatican Council called for a "return to the authentic sources" as a well-spring from which guidance and wisdom could be drawn to assist in the great work of spreading the gospel of Christ in the modern world. In response to this call, there has been a renewed interest in early Church history, as well as the writings of the ancient Fathers of the Church. This has been evident particularly in the United States since the mid-1980s, as well as in other parts of the English-speaking world, including Australia.

The Church has had a long and chequered history. It is a history that is remote and unknown to most people today, including many Catholics. *The Lord of History Series* attempts to give an introduction to the early centuries of that history systematically through easy-to-read short chapters.

Volume I covers the first four centuries of Church history immediately following the period outlined in the *Acts of the Apostles*. It is an age of much drama, growth and suffering for the Church. There are many heroes, villains and controversies. We are introduced to the martyrs, saints and heroes who helped to expand the foundations of the Church, as well as the first great theologians, apologists and biblical exegetes. The Gospel of Christ is advancing, but in the face of official opposition and persecution. The various heresies are presented, together with the responses these elicited from the Church. The ultimate triumph of the Church is dealt with the chapters concerning the rise of Constantine, which are followed by a treatment of the great theological and Christological controversies of the fourth and fifth centuries. It is all stirring reading for the novice in Church history and a thorough introduction for those who want to pursue serious studies in this area.

Volume II is more specialised, looking at thirty of the most famous Fathers of the Church. The study of the Fathers is of perennial benefit to the Church and the faithful. These were men of undoubted sanctity and learning, whose writings contributed greatly to the authentic development of doctrine in those same early centuries. Many of the Fathers were also saints or martyrs, or even Doctors of the Church. Theirs is a wisdom that can never be dispensed with, a deep well from which new and old things can always be drawn. Again, in a simple and easy-to-read format, each chapter in this volume provides a basic biography of the Father in question, followed by a selection of individual quotes form their writings, carefully chosen to highlight the Catholic nature of their faith, and to illustrate that the early Church is the one same Holy Catholic Church we, by grace of God, belong to today.

Yours sincerely,

Dr George Pell
Archbishop of Sydney   1 August 2003

Index

Foreword v

1. Introduction 1

AD 30 to AD 100: THE ACTS OF THE APOSTLES

2. Pentecost Day and Afterwards 4
3. The Conversion of St Paul 8
4. The Dispersion of the Apostles 11
5. The Early Missions of Sts Peter and Paul 15
6. The Missions of Sts Jude and Thomas 21
7. The Council of Jerusalem 26
8. The Later Missions of Sts Peter and Paul 30
9. The Neronian Persecution 33
10. The Jewish Revolt AD 66-70 39
11. The Church in the Late First Century AD 44
12. St John the Apostle 50

AD 101 to AD 200: THE APOSTOLIC FATHERS AND APOLOGISTS

13. Sts Ignatius of Antioch and Polycarp of Smyrna 54
14. Hermas and St Justin Martyr 61
15. St Irenaeus of Lyons and the Gnostic Heresy 66
16. The Catechetical School of Alexandria 72

AD 201 to AD 300: THE PERSECUTIONS AND THE POPES

17. Heresy and Schism in the Pontificate of St Callistus I 78
18. The Persecutions of Maximinus Thrax and Decius 83
19. Pope St Stephen I and St Cyprian of Carthage 87
20. The Persecutions of Valerian and Aurelian 91

AD 301 to AD 400: THE TRIUMPH OF THE CROSS AND OF ORTHODOXY

21. The Diocletian Persecution	95
22. The Ascendancy of Constantine	100
23. The Triumph of Constantine	103
24. The Donatist Heresy	108
25. Arianism and the Council of Nicaea	112
26. The Post-Nicene Struggle	116
27. The Triumph of Orthodoxy	122

AD 401 to AD 476: THE GREATEST OF THE FATHERS AND THE FALL OF ROME

28. The Genius of St Augustine of Hippo	128
29. The Nestorian and Monophysite Heresies	135
30. The Barbarian Invasions up to AD 476	141

Appendices

Appendix A: Popes of the Early Church AD 30-476	145
Appendix B: Roman Emperors from the Time of Christ to AD 476	146
Appendix C: Creeds of the Early Church 1st- 5th centuries AD	147
Acknowledgments	155
About the Author	157
Other Works by the Author	158

Introduction

Jesus Christ is Lord of History. Despite the fact that the vast majority of contemporary historians ignore His life and work, no other figure can claim to have altered the course of history more than the humble carpenter from Nazareth.

The moment of Christ's entry into the world was no simple accident or coincidence, but ordained by God in His good time: "But when the fullness of time had come, God sent his Son, born of a woman, born under the law, in order to redeem those who were under the law, so that we might receive adoption as children." The reading from the *Roman Martyrology* for the 25th of December wonderfully places the birth of Christ in the context of human history:

> In the year, from the creation of the world, when in the beginning God created heaven and earth, five thousand one hundred and ninety-nine; from the flood, two thousand nine hundred and fifty-seven; from the birth of Abraham, two thousand and fifteen; from Moses and the coming of the Israelites out of Egypt, one thousand five hundred and ten; from the anointing of King David, one thousand and thirty-two; in the sixty-fifth week, according to the prophecy of Daniel; in the one hundred and ninety-fourth Olympiad; in the year seven hundred and fifty-two from the founding of the city of Rome; in the forty-second year of the empire of Octavian Augustus, when the whole world was at peace, in the sixth age of the world, Jesus Christ, eternal God, and Son of the eternal Father, desirous to sanctify the world by His most merciful coming, having been conceived by the Holy Spirit, and nine months having elapsed since His conception, is born in Bethlehem of Juda, having become Man of the Virgin Mary.

At the time of Christ's coming, most of the known world was dominated by Rome under her first Emperor, Augustus Caesar. Before the rise of Rome there had been Sumer, Egypt, the Hittites, Assyria, Babylon, Persia, Greece and Alexander the Great. Rome was the empire of iron, greater in extent than all the others, making the Mediterranean her *"mare nostrum."* What would come after Rome? The kingdom that "is not of this world." The Babe from Bethlehem would determine that, but not before 248 years of deadly struggle between those who followed Him as the true God-man, and those who followed the Emperors as the false ones.

This work is a basic introduction designed to study the earliest history of the Church with a particular view to discovering those outstanding events and persons who laid the foundations of Christendom for the next one thousand five hundred years. We will also see that it is a history thoroughly Catholic from its very beginnings. Some of the greatest converts to Catholicism over the last five hundred years attributed their conversion to their study of the early Church, particularly the writings of the Fathers – e.g., St Edmund Campion and John Henry Cardinal Newman. They saw that the Catholic Church was the Church of the first three centuries and that all its teachings can be found either explicitly or implicitly in the writings of this period: *"The Christianity of history is not Protestantism. If ever there was a safe truth it is this, and Protestantism has ever felt it so. To be deep in history is to cease to be a Protestant* (John Henry Cardinal Newman – *An Essay on the Development of Christian Doctrine*).

The years between AD 30 and AD 476 are filled with great adventure, courage, tragedy and triumph. It opens with the missionary work of the Apostles, particular the work of Sts Peter, Paul and Thomas. The dispersion of the Apostles in AD 42 would see the spreading of Christianity throughout the Roman and Parthian Empires, across even to India. Reactions would follow, including the execution of St James the Greater and the expulsion of all Christians and Jews from Rome in AD 49.

The full-scale persecution of Christianity would be started by the megalomaniac Nero, seeking scapegoats for his insane burning of Rome in AD 64. This persecution would claim the lives of Sts Peter and Paul, as well as thousands of innocent Christian souls. After his assassination, only one law of Nero's would remain – the edict outlawing Christianity. Persecution after persecution would follow: Domitian, Trajan, Marcus Aurelius, Septimus Severus, Thrax, Decius, Valerian, Aurelian and Diocletian would over the next 245 years all tread down the same road as Nero, and all achieve the same vain results. Despite each persecution, the Church of Christ would continue to grow: *"The blood of the martyrs is the seed of the Church."* Martyrs multiplied, but so did converts, while old Rome grew tired and desperately tried to regain her former glory. As persecuted

Introduction

Popes went to their glorious deaths, persecuting Emperors found death, assassination or insanity (and even the occasional lightning bolt!).

During the age of persecution, early Fathers and Apologists would write the first pieces of Christian literature outside the canonical Scriptures. The value of their writings was matched by both the value of their lives and their martyrdoms. Sts Ignatius, Polycarp and Justin resound from the second century, Irenaeus and Clement of Alexandria from the early third. As Rome decayed further, more frequent would be the persecutions. Bishops, Priests and Deacons – none would be spared the sword, whip, rack or roast. Young virgins, old men, even the Scriptures and sacred vessels would feed the flames. Heroes abounded, but so did apostates. It will always be easier to speak of martyrs than to die as one.

"In Thee, Lord, we place our trust. We shall never be put to shame." That trust in the Lord would not be in vain. While the Church endured her tenth and so far greatest persecution from the Tetrarchs Diocletian, Galerius, Maximian and Daia, a doubtful Constantine contemplated seizing Rome from the tyrants. The haruspices said no, but the cross and the words in the sky said yes: *"In Hoc Signo Vinces."* The battle was fought nine miles outside of Rome, and on 29 October, AD 312, Constantine's labarum with the letters Chi-Rho entered the ancient capital of the Empire in triumph.

And so would begin a new era – the liberty of the Church. It would be a springtime of Church construction and mass conversion. But he who "goes about seeking the ruin of souls" never sleeps and heresy would be his next weapon. Donatus, Arius, Nestorius and Eutyches would plant their seeds of doubt and division. In response, Councils, Creeds, Saints and Fathers would rise to meet the challenge. New heroes of colossal stature would appear: Athanasius, Ambrose, Hilary, Basil, Chrysostom and Augustine – just to name a few. So, too, new types of Christian heroism – the hermitical and monastic lifestyles.

From liberty to establishment – Christianity would become the official religion of the Roman Empire in AD 380. But it was an Empire in its death-throws. Not even a growing Church and new Christian civil laws could save it. Finally overwhelmed by the barbarians, it would be carved up and fade into romantic memory. To some it seemed the end of the world; but unbeknown to the carnal eye, it was really the beginning of a new one. This new world would be a fruit of the Tree that once stood on Calvary.

AD 30 to AD 100: THE ACTS OF THE APOSTLES

Pentecost Day and Afterwards

On 19 May, AD 30, the Virgin Mary, the surviving Apostles and one hundred and twenty others watched Jesus Christ ascend into Heaven from Mt. Olivet.[1] Afterwards, these same people, constituting the infant Church, retired to the 'upper room', or Cenacle, to await the coming of the "new Advocate" promised by Jesus: "... for John baptized with water, but before many days you shall be baptized with the Holy Spirit."

Nine days later, Pentecost Sunday, 29 May, He came. Pentecost was a festival of great importance for the Jews. It celebrated the giving of the Law and the end of the harvest season. Some weeks earlier, in the same room Christ had spoken of "the new and everlasting covenant" and offered His Body to eat and His Blood to drink. Now a new Law was being instituted and a new harvest about to begin:

> When the day of Pentecost had come, they were all together in one place. And suddenly a sound came from heaven like the rush of a mighty wind, and it filled all the house where they were sitting. And there appeared to them tongues as of fire, distributed and resting on each one of them. And they were all filled with the Holy

---

[1] See Warren H. Carroll, *The Founding of Christendom* (A History of Christendom), Vol. 1, Christendom Press, 1985, pp. 394. This date would have the crucifixion of Christ occurring on Friday, 7 April.

Spirit and began to speak in other tongues, as the Spirit gave them utterance" (Acts 2:1-4).

There were many Jews in Jerusalem at this time from the countries of the Diaspora (dispersion) who, hearing the noise of the strong driving wind, gathered in a crowd around the Cenacle. They were from Pontus, Phrygia, Pamphylia, Cappodocia, Cyrene, Parthia, Media, Arabia, Crete, Greece and Rome – all Jews or Jewish converts. They all saw those inside the Cenacle moving and swaying, and heard them speaking in their own languages about the great things that God had done. Some thought that they had had their fill of new wine. Filled instead with the gifts of the Holy Spirit, St Peter emerged to address the astonished crowd of onlookers:

> And in the last days it shall be, God declares, that I will pour out my Spirit upon all flesh, and your sons and your daughters shall prophesy, and your young men shall see visions, and your old men shall dream dreams ... This Jesus God raised up, and of that we all are witnesses. Being therefore exalted at the right hand of God, and having received from the Father the promise of the Holy Spirit, he has poured out this which you see and hear ... Let all the house of Israel therefore know assuredly that God has made him both Lord and Christ, this Jesus whom you crucified (Acts 2:17-33).

The force of St Peter's words was irresistible. His listeners were "cut to the heart" and asked, "Brethren, what shall we do?" "Repent, and be baptized every one of you in the name of Jesus Christ for the forgiveness of your sins ..." By the end of that day alone, three thousand new members had been baptized into the Church. Within a few days it would be five thousand. Many of these were from those pilgrims of the dispersion, who would soon return to their countries with their new faith. The conversion of the world had begun!: "...and you shall be my witnesses in Jerusalem and in all Judea and Samaria and to the end of the earth."

Day by day the early Christians "devoted themselves to the apostles' teaching and fellowship, to the breaking of bread and the prayers" (Acts 2:42). They shared all things in common and each day the "the Lord added to their number ... those who were being saved." Annoyed, the Jewish priests of the Temple and the Sadducees felt compelled to intervene. Sts Peter and John were arrested and ordered "not to speak or teach at all in the name of Jesus." But they answered, "Whether it is right in the sight of God to listen to you rather than to God." Arrested a second time for continuing to preach in the name of Jesus, the High Priest would have had them killed, but Gamaliel, one of the Pharisees held in honor by all the people spoke thus: "... tell you, keep away from these men and let them alone; for if this plan or this undertaking is of men, it will fail; but if it is of God, you will not be able to overthrow them." Gamaliel's advice was taken, and Sts Peter and John were scourged and set free: "then they left the presence of the Council rejoicing that they were counted worthy to suffer dishonor for the name of Jesus."

As the Church grew in Jerusalem and Palestine, the need arose to appoint the first new members to the Church hierarchy other than the Apostles. Already, Matthias had been chosen by lot to replace Judas Iscariot. Now, hands would be laid on seven deacons (Greek: *Diakonein* – to minister) to serve the spiritual and temporal needs of the Greek-speaking Christians (or Hellenists). One of these seven was St Stephen.

St Stephen, "full of grace and power, did great wonders and signs among the people." He also prophesied boldly about the near future, how the Law of Moses would be supplanted and the Temple one day laid waste. The Jewish authorities moved in, arresting St Stephen and charging him with blasphemy. Before the High Priest and the Council St Stephen declared, "You stiff-necked people, uncircumcised in heart and ears, you always resist the Holy Spirit. As your fathers did, so do you ... the Righteous One, whom you have now betrayed and murdered, you who received the law as delivered by angels and did not keep it." In furious anger, the Jews threatened him, and he cried out, "I see the heavens opened, and the Son of man standing at the right hand of God." Abandoning all pretense of legality, the Jews dragged St Stephen outside the city and stoned him to death. As he fell he prayed, "Lord, do not hold this sin against them." The Church had its first martyr.

Watching all this in approval was a young Jew from Tarsus. He stood nearby and held the garments of the Council members so that they might better throw the stones. His name was Saul.

Themes for study:
- The descent of the Holy Spirit on Pentecost Day.
- The rapid growth of the early Church.
- The reaction of the Jewish authorities.
- Sts Peter, John and Stephen as proto-confessors and proto-martyr respectively.

Further reading:
- *Acts of the Apostles*, chapters 1-7.
- *The Catholic Encyclopaedia* (1911, vol. XIV, pp. 286-287).
- Warren H. Carroll, *The Founding of Christendom* (A History of Christendom), Vol. 1, Christendom Press, 1985, pp. 394-398.
- Fr John Laux, *Church History*, TAN Books and Publishers, 1930, pp. 7-11.

The Conversion of St Paul

The martyrdom of St Stephen was the signal for a concerted and widespread persecution of the Church: "... on that day a great persecution arose against the church in Jerusalem; and they were all scattered throughout the region of Judea and Samaria, except the apostles."

While Rome ruled Jerusalem, the Jews themselves could not carry out the death penalty, thus inhibiting their efforts to destroy the "sect of the Nazarene." However, unexpectedly, there would open a brief window of opportunity. The Emperor Tiberius died in AD 37 and his successor, Caligula, had yet to appoint a replacement for the Governor, Pontius Pilate. Further, the lacunae in Roman governorship would enable the Jewish leaders to extend their planned persecution against Christians living immediately outside Judea.

One Jewish Christian community to be targeted was the Church in Damascus, Syria. No ordinary Jew could be trusted for such an important mission. So the High Priest granted Saul the necessary letters of authority. Saul was of the tribe of Benjamin but a native of Hellenistic Tarsus in Cilicia and a Roman citizen. He was present at the martyrdom of St Stephen and watched with great approval. He was the "Pharisee of Pharisees" having studied under Gamaliel, and fervently and honestly abhorred the followers of the Nazarene as enemies of God and destroyers of the Jewish Law. He had already zealously sought them out in Jerusalem and volunteered to pursue the fugitives who had escaped to Syria. In mid AD 37, Saul set forth along the road to Damascus, "still breathing threats and murder against the disciples of the Lord." The Acts of the Apostles relates what happened next:

> Now as he journeyed he approached Damascus, and suddenly a light from heaven flashed about him. And he fell to the ground and heard a voice saying to him, "Saul, Saul, why do you persecute me?" And he said, "Who are you, Lord?" And he said, "I am Jesus, whom you are persecuting; but rise and enter the city, and you will be told what you are to do" (9:3-6).

Saul could both hear and see Jesus; his traveling companions could only hear Him. Saul was brought to a house in Damascus on Straight Street and for the next three days could not see, eat or drink. During this time, he received a vision of a man named Ananias coming to lay hands on him to cure him. Ananias when told by Jesus to visit Saul hesitated, but was then told, "Go, for he is a chosen instrument of mine to carry my name before the Gentiles and kings and the sons of Israel." Saul's vision soon came to pass, and Ananias cured him of his blindness and then baptized him. Saul the persecutor was now St Paul the disciple. The significance of his conversion can never be overstated:

> To the Church in that hour was given the personality which more than any other has shaped its thought, its organization, its spirit; the greatest of converts, the greatest of disciples, greatest of missionaries, thinker, ascetic, mystic, the follower in whom more than in any other is mirrored the Master.[1]

In the days that immediately followed, St Paul was seen in the synagogues of Damascus proclaiming Jesus as the Son of God. Jews and Christians alike were amazed declaring, "Is not this the man who made havoc in Jerusalem of those who called on this name?" St Paul became even bolder, confuting those Jews who challenged him. Eventually, St Paul retired to the desert of Arabia (possibly somewhere in Sinai) and during the next three years prepared himself through prayer, contemplation and study of the Old Testament Scriptures for his future mission.

Returning first to Damascus, St Paul once more sought to convert the Jews to the belief that Jesus "is the Son of God." In order to silence him this time, the Jews plotted St Paul's death, waiting to ambush him as he left through the gates of Damascus. Knowing of the plot, disciples of St Paul lowered him down the walls of the city at night, allowing him to escape and make his way to Jerusalem.

In Jerusalem, St Paul sought to make himself known to St Peter and the other Apostles, however, they at first did not believe that he was a true disciple and sought to avoid him. It was another Hellenist Jewish convert, St Barnabas, who vouched for his conversion and his preaching in the name of Jesus at Damascus. After spending fifteen days with St Peter in

---

[1] Philip Hughes, *A History of the Church*, Vol. 1, Sheed and Ward, 1948, p. 43.

Jerusalem, St Paul began to dispute with the Hellenist Jews and, once again, found his life under threat. Knowing of this new Jewish intrigue, St Paul was forced to retire a second time and was brought to Caesarea and shipped to Tarsus. It seemed as though the Jews would always succeed in frustrating his work. At about this time a vision of Jesus consoled St Paul, confirming his future mission among the Gentiles: "I will send you far away to the Gentiles." St Paul remained in Tarsus for the next five to six years, unseen and unheard, until St Barnabas ventures in search of him.

Themes for study:
- The conversion of Saul to St Paul.
- St Paul as Christ's chosen instrument to carry His name before the Gentiles and kings and the sons of Israel.
- The plots arranged against St Paul's life by the Jews.
- His acceptance by the Apostles as a true disciple.

Further reading:
- *Acts of the Apostles*, chapter 9.
- Warren H. Carroll, *The Founding of Christendom* (A History of Christendom), Vol. 1, Christendom Press, 1985, pp. 398-399.
- Philip Hughes, *A History of the Church*, Vol. 1, Sheed and Ward, 1948, pp. 43-44.
- Fr John Laux, *Church History*, TAN Books and Publishers, 1930, pp. 11-12.

The Dispersion of the Apostles

Despite the intrigues against St Paul, the missionary work of the infant Church continued apace. In Acts 8 we read of the conversion and baptism of the Jewish – Ethiopian eunuch ("a minister of Candace, queen of the Ethiopians") by the Deacon Philip. There is a tradition that St Matthew followed this eunuch to Ethiopia some years afterwards. Three hundred years later, Christian missionaries venturing into the Upper Nile region would find people aware of the sign of the Cross.[1]

In AD 39, St Peter was traveling along the Palestinian coastal plain confirming and strengthening neophytes converted by Deacon Philip. The most important city then in the region was Caesarea with its artificial harbor and Roman cohort. One member of this cohort was the centurion Cornelius, a friend and benefactor of the Jews. While at his regular prayer, Cornelius received an unexpected visitor, and angel of God who commanded him to dispatch men and bring St Peter who was at that time in Joppa. Reassured by the Holy Spirit, St Peter made his way to Caesarea, where he saw the Holy Spirit descend upon Cornelius' pagan household. St Peter then declared, "Can anyone forbid water for baptizing these people who have received the Holy Spirit just as we have?" The Church had received her first Gentile converts:

> "The Church, from this day, ceased to be a Jewish community; 'it will be an international society where shall meet as brothers, without distinction of rite or race, the Jew and the Gentile, the master and the slave, the poor and the rich. In vain does Israel promise herself the first place in the kingdom of God. Israel can disappear without causing a vacuum; her mission is ended and her place henceforth will be taken by a spiritual Israel made up of all the faithful.'"[2]

---

[1] Warren H. Carroll, *The Founding of Christendom*, ibid., p. 400.
[2] Fr John Laux, *Church History*, TAN Books and Publishers, 1930, p. 14.

The conversion of Cornelius would trigger a flood of Gentile converts into the Church. Greek-speaking Jewish Christians, hearing of what happened in Caesarea, would begin preaching Christ in Antioch in northern Syria. Antioch at this time was a thriving cosmopolitan hub of over half a million inhabitants, the third largest city in the Empire behind only Rome and Alexandria. Such was their success that St Barnabas was sent from Jerusalem to take control of this new mission. Antioch has the great distinction of being the first place where the followers of Jesus were called Christians (Acts 11:26).

However, all this success in the name of Christ would soon face a new and dangerous threat. The Emperor Caligula, lost in his insanity and self-worship, was assassinated by the Praetorian Guards in January AD 41. His successor, Claudius, was favorable to the Jews and awarded Herod Agrippa (the grandson of Herod the Great) virtual independent rule over Judea and Samaria. Agrippa held some favor with the Jewish religious leadership as he had recently used his friendship with Caligula to forestall the erection of a statue of himself in the Temple of Jerusalem. This new political reality exposed the Christian community to grave dangers, for their Jewish enemies could count on Agrippa's help in applying traditional Mosaic capital punishments against them.

So it was that early in AD 42 the Apostles made the momentous decision of dispersing. The Master had warned them of persecution, and now His words were about to come to pass:

> I have said all this to you to keep you from falling away. They will put you out of the synagogues; indeed, the hour is coming when whoever kills you will think he is offering service to God. And they will do this because they have not known the Father, nor me (John 16:1-3).

But this was not to be a dispersion simply to avoid persecution, rather more the compliance with Christ's command to be His witnesses "to the ends of the earth." It was meticulously planned, having in view the great distances to be traveled in and outside the Roman Empire and the needs of the remaining Church in Jerusalem. Sts Peter, James the Greater, John and James the Less ("the Lord's brother") would remain in Jerusalem, with Hebrew and Greek copies of the first written record of Christ's life, death and resurrection — the Gospel of St Matthew. According to the scanty traditions we possess, the other Apostles dispersed as follows:

St Andrew — central Ukraine and Greece;

St Bartholomew — southern Arabia (perhaps also India);

St Jude — Mesopotamia (perhaps also Armenia and Iran);

St Matthew — Ethiopia (or perhaps Iran around the Caspian Sea);

St Matthias — unknown;

St Philip — Phrygia in Asia Minor;

St Simon the Zealot — Iran;

St Thomas — Parthia, northern and southern India, and the island of Socotra.

The Apostles' fear of danger from Agrippa would prove true. Just before the Passover of AD 42, St James the Greater was arrested and beheaded to please the Jews, becoming the first Apostle-martyr for Christ. St John would go into hiding (with the Blessed Mother) to re-emerge later in Ephesus in Asia Minor. Soon after, St Peter was also imprisoned, only to be miraculously freed by an angel. Acts tells us that St Peter then "departed and went to another place" (12:17). What was this other place? The head of the Apostles had made the most momentous move in the history of the early Church — he departed from Jerusalem with the aim of reaching the capital of the Empire, Rome. It was inevitable that the leader of the Church on earth would make his way to the leading city in the world. On his way he stayed for some time in Antioch, reorganizing the Church there and transferring the leadership from St Barnabas to the pagan convert Evodius.

Passing through Asia Minor, St Peter probably arrived in Rome just before the end of AD 42. It is believed he stayed among the Jews of the Fourteenth District, which stretched along the Tiber and included Vatican

Hill. There were probably also Christian converts living in Rome from Pentecost Day. St Peter is now Bishop of Rome, unknown and unnoticed by the one million or so inhabitants of the world's premier city. There, he would set a pattern of apostolic work that would be repeated many times over by St Paul: preach first to the Jews with limited success, and then turn to the Gentiles for the richer harvest. The Roman historian Tacitus[3] tells us of one such Gentile convert, Pomponia Graecina, the wife of the Roman General Aulus Plautinus, who is said to have adopted an "unknown superstition", to which she remained faithful for over the next forty years.

Themes for study:
- The first Gentile converts.
- The establishment and growth of the Church in Antioch.
- The dispersion of the Apostles throughout and beyond the Roman Empire.
- St Peter's arrival in Rome.

Further reading:
- *Acts of the Apostles*, chapters 10-12.
- Warren H. Carroll, *The Founding of Christendom* (A History of Christendom), Vol. 1, Christendom Press, 1985, pp. 400-407.
- Fernard Hayward, *A History of the Popes*, J.M. Dent & Sons Ltd., 1931, pp. 7-9.
- Fr John Laux, *Church History*, TAN Books and Publishers, 1930, pp. 13-15.

---

[3] *Annales*, XIII, 32.

The Early Missions of Sts Peter and Paul

Undisturbed in Rome, St Peter's apostolate would begin to reap a rich harvest. Meanwhile, back in Jerusalem, political developments would again take a sudden turn. It is said that pride comes before the fall – and this saying was to dramatically prove true in the case of Herod Agrippa. While in Caesarea in early AD 44, Agrippa received a delegation from the people of Tyre and Sidon who came intent on being reconciled to him as they depended on the King's country for food. Agrippa put on his finest robes, ascended his throne, and began to harangue the delegation. Acts tells us that some in the delegation began to shout out, "The voice of a god, and not of man!" Immediately, Agrippa was struck down by an angel "because he did not give God the glory" (12:20-23). He was eaten up by worms and died five days afterwards. The great Jewish historian Josephus records the event in similar fashion, adding some extra spice:

> Herod Agrippa was exhibiting shows in Caesarea in honor of Claudius. On the second day of the shows he put on a garment made wholly of silver, of wonderful contexture, and came into the theater early in the morning. There the silver, lit up by the beating of the sun's first rays upon it, shone forth marvelously, and by its flashing cast a fear and terror upon those who gazed at him. And straightway his flatterers cried out, one from one place, and another from another, not for his good, addressing him as a god; and they added, 'Deal kindly with us; if hitherto we have revered thee as a man, yet henceforth we confess thee superior to mortal nature.' The King rebuked them not, nor rejected their impious flattery. A great pain arose in his belly, from the outset most violent. Looking, therefore, upon his friends, he said, 'I, your god, am now bidden depart this life, for so Providence confutes the lying words even now spoken of me; and I, who was by you called immortal, am now hurried away to death.[1]

---

[1] *Jewish Antiquities*, XIX, 8.

Herod Agrippa was the last "King of the Jews." The Roman Procurator, Cuspius Fadus, succeeded him in AD 45. A period of peace would now begin for the Church lasting twenty years. These years would witness the great missionary efforts of Sts Peter and Paul.

St Paul was, coincidently, in Jerusalem at the time of Agrippa's death. He had been brought out of the obscurity of Tarsus by St Barnabas to assist in the evangelization of Antioch and now both were in Jerusalem bringing aid to the Church there suffering under Agrippa's persecution. They returned together to Antioch in AD 45, bringing from Jerusalem St Barnabas' cousin, John Mark (aka St Mark). It was while back in Antioch that St Paul received another decisive call from heaven, one from the Holy Spirit that would launch him on the greatest evangelization mission in the history of the early Church: "Set apart for me Barnabas and Saul for the work to which I have called them." After having hands laid upon them, Sts Paul and Barnabas (now having the rank of Bishops), along with St Mark, were "sent ... off."

St Paul's first missionary journey had begun. The first port of call was St Barnabas' homeland, Cyprus. They crossed the whole island, preaching mostly to the local Jewish communities. From Cyprus, the gallant missionaries crossed into Asia Minor, preaching Christ in the following regions: Pamphylia, Antioch in Pisidia, Iconium, Lystra and Derbe in Lycaonia. There were notable successes: the Roman Proconsul of Cyprus, Sergius Paulus, "learned to believe"; a flourishing Gentile Christian community was established in Antioch in Pisidia; and in Lystra, St Paul met his future dear friend and disciple St Timothy. In all, seven infant churches were planted. There were also some disappointments and failures: St Mark abandoned the journey at the foot of the Taurus Mountains before Antioch in Pisidia; the Jews of the same city rejected St Paul's preaching and cursed him; in Lystra, both St Paul and St Barnabas narrowly escaped being worshipped as gods; and again in Lystra St Paul was stoned and left for dead by a mob enraged by Jewish intrigue. By the time St Paul and St Barnabas had returned to Antioch in Syria it was AD 49. The journey had taken four years.

It was while on his first journey that St Paul uttered the following words to the Jews:

> It was necessary that the word of God should be spoken first to you. Since you thrust it from you, and judge yourselves

unworthy of eternal life, behold, we turn to the Gentiles. For so the Lord has commanded us, saying, "I have set you to be a light for the Gentiles, that you may bring salvation to the uttermost parts of the earth."

In all the other missionary journeys of St Paul the same pattern would be repeated: an initial preaching to the Jews resulting in limited success and general rejection, followed by a turning to the Gentiles and a more fruitful harvest in the midst of continued Jewish harassment and intrigue.

Meanwhile, back in Rome St Peter continued to work steadily building the Church in the capital of the Empire. His success, however, was under threat from two fronts. Firstly, the Emperor Claudius was becoming concerned about the growth of "foreign cults" and from AD 47 engaged in a campaign to restore the traditional Roman rites. Secondly, the preaching of the Gospel aroused the usual disturbances from the Jews. These disturbances were of a type similar to those raised against St Paul, and were significant enough to be brought to the attention of the Emperor. Seizing on these disturbances as a pretext, and thinking that they were simply squabbles between co-religious, Claudius in AD 49 ordered the expulsion of all Jews from Rome: *"Judaeos impulsore Chresto assidue tumultuantes Roma expulit."*[2] St Peter could no longer remain in the eternal city, and we find him in Jerusalem again by late AD 49. Also leaving Rome were the Jewish Christians Aquila and Priscilla, who were later to team up with St Paul in Corinth. There is some conjecture that these two were converted by St Peter, and were asked to remain in Corinth by the Fisherman to continue working with the infant Church he planted there while on his return journey to Jerusalem.[3]

The hand of Providence may well have led the head of the Church back to Jerusalem at this time for another reason. Tradition tells us that the Mother of God, hitherto in the precious care of the Apostle John for the last nineteen years, was about to 'fall asleep' in the Lord. Another tradition tells us that all the Apostles still living at the time were

---

[2] Suetonius, *Lives of the Caesars*, Claud. 25:4: "He expelled the Jews from Rome, since, stirred up by Chrestus, they were continually causing disturbances."

[3] 1 Cor. 1:12 infers that certain Christians in Corinth certainly had personal knowledge of St Peter.

miraculously translated from their mission fields and brought to Jerusalem to be at her bedside and to witness her Assumption into Heaven. Certainly, Sts Peter, John, James the Less and Paul were in the great city, and Acts tells us that at the subsequent Council of Jerusalem "the Apostles and elders were gathered together" (15:6).

> To picture Mary, the Mother of God, tenderly taking leave of her first and dearest spiritual children, the Apostles, on the eve of the Apostolic Council, is an entrancing vision; to date her Assumption then is magnificently appropriate. The dating and the occasion cannot be said to be historically provable in the fragmentary condition of our evidence, though it is both reasonable and likely; the Assumption itself — defined as infallible dogma by the Roman Catholic Church — is strongly indicated historically by the absence of any tradition of a burial place of the Blessed Virgin Mary or any veneration of relics thought to be hers, combined with the tradition of her 'falling asleep' in Jerusalem.[4]

Soon after the conclusion of the Council of Jerusalem, Sts Peter and Paul met together in Antioch. It was here and now (AD 50) that the famous face-to-face clash recounted by St Paul in his letter to the Galatians occurred between the two. St Peter, overawed by a delegation of 'Judaizers' from Jerusalem still insisting that all converts to the Church observe the law of Moses, ceased eating with the Gentile converts. Noticing this behavior, St Paul "opposed him to his face" (2:11). In doing this, he was simply reminding St Peter of his own words, approved in the Council, not to put "a yoke upon the neck of the disciples which neither our fathers nor we have been able to bear." Realizing both his weakness to human respect and error, St Peter acknowledged the correction.

Unable to return to Rome while Claudius lived, St Peter made Antioch his base for missionary work in northern Asia Minor. For four years until AD 54, he evangelized Bithynia, Pontus and Cappadocia, establishing Christian churches that would grow into large communities by the end of the first century.[5] St Peter's first epistle, written after AD 62

---

[4] Warren H. Carroll, *The Founding of Christendom*, ibid., p. 414.
[5] Pliny the Younger, in his letter to the Emperor Trajan (Ep. X, 96, c. AD 111) stated that, "many people of all ages, from every walk of life are endangered and will continue to be so."

from Rome (under the code-name "Babylon"), was addressed to the Christians of these regions.

St Paul's second missionary journey would be launched again from Antioch but start with a dramatic fallout between long-time partners. St Barnabas insisted on bringing along St Mark but St Paul, remembering how St Mark abandoned them at the foot of the Taurus Mountains, refused to have him. Therefore, they decided to part company: St Barnabas and St Mark to Cyprus[6]; St Paul and Silas into Asia Minor.

St Paul aimed, initially, to revisit the communities founded during his first journey, strengthening them in the Faith. At Iconium, St Paul and Silas joined with the half-Jew/half-Gentile St Timothy, and the three traveled across to Troas on the western coast of Asia Minor (along the way, St Paul was warned by "the Spirit of Jesus" not to enter Bithynia). There, the "beloved physician" St Luke joined them, and St Paul received a vision of a Macedonian imploring them to come and preach the Gospel: "Come over to Macedonia and help us." Arriving in Philippi, they made many converts, including Lydia of Thyatira, "a seller of purple goods, who was a worshiper of God." While in Philippi, St Paul and Silas were arrested, beaten with rods and imprisoned. When it was realized that they were both Roman citizens, the two were released with apologies. Leaving the Philippian church in the hands of Sts Timothy and Luke, St Paul and Silas continued to Thessalonica where St Paul preached for three weeks, gaining notable converts, until the intrigue of the Jews caught up with them again at the expense of their host, Jason, and other converts who were attacked, dragged into the street and accused of declaring that there was another King besides Caesar, namely Jesus.

Safely escaping to nearby Beroea, St Paul and Silas preached with even greater success among the locals who "received the word with all eagerness", until St Paul alone was forced out again by the Jews from Thessalonica and onto a ship bound for Athens. In the capital of the Hellenic world, St Paul spoke to the Jews in the synagogue and debated with Epicurean and Stoic philosophers. While waiting for Silas and St Timothy to join him, St Paul made his famous speech before the

---

[6] St Barnabas would remain on Cyprus for the rest of his life, becoming its first Bishop; St Mark would later attach himself to St Peter and found the Church in Alexandria, Egypt.

philosophers in the Areopagus, proclaiming the "unknown God": "What therefore you worship as unknown, this I proclaim to you." The "babbler", as they called him, made some converts, including Dionysius the Areopagite, later the first Bishop of Athens. From philosophical Athens, St Paul moved on to sensual Corinth (the center of the worship of Aphrodite), staying at the house of Aquila and Priscilla. Crispus, the leader of the local synagogue, was converted, though the majority of Jews again held back and had St Paul brought before the Roman Governor, Gallio, who, however, refused to interfere in a matter of religion. It was while in Corinth that Jesus appeared to St Paul in a vision, encouraging him to remain bold in his preaching: "Do not be afraid, but speak and do not be silent; for I am with you ... I have many people in this city." Also while in Corinth St Paul wrote his first two epistles, the letters to the Thessalonians, during the winter of AD 51-52, probably in response to questions brought by Silas. From Corinth, St Paul and Silas sailed to Ephesus and then to Caesarea in Palestine. Passing through and greeting the Church in Jerusalem, they returned to Antioch. It was now late AD 52.

Themes for study:
- The death of Herod Agrippa.
- The Assumption of the Blessed Virgin Mary.
- St Peter's expulsion from Rome and his work in northern Asia Minor.
- St Paul's first and second missionary journeys.

Further reading:
- *Acts of the Apostles*, chapters 12-18.
- Warren H. Carroll, *The Founding of Christendom* (A History of Christendom), Vol. 1, Christendom Press, 1985, pp. 411-417.
- Fernard Hayward, *A History of the Popes*, J.M. Dent & Sons Ltd., 1931, pp. 9-12.
- Philip Hughes, *A History of the Church*, Vol. 1, Sheed and Ward, 1948, pp. 45-48.

The Missions of Sts Jude and Thomas

Of all the Apostles besides Sts Peter and Paul, we only possess sufficient evidence to reconstruct the missionary activities of two others — Sts Jude and Thomas.

An ancient Syriac document called *The Teaching of Addai* dating from the late third, perhaps early fourth century AD, tells of a man named Addai, sent by Jesus to King Abgar the Black of Edessa, in north—western Mesopotamia. King Abgar had been stricken with leprosy, and hearing of the miraculous cures of Jesus, sent a message to Him imploring a cure. Jesus received the plea, and responded saying that He could not come Himself as His mission was to the Jews only, but that after He had returned to His Father He would send one of His disciples.

More than ten years after the Ascension, the promised disciple, named Addai, would arrive, bearing with him a mysterious picture of Christ on a cloth that had been "doubled in four." This 'picture' in all probability was the so-called Shroud of Turin, found by Sts Peter and John in the tomb of Christ on the day of His resurrection. It not only showed the face of Christ, but His whole body, front and back, together with the wounds and blood from His passion and crucifixion. The Apostles had hitherto kept this precious relic under wraps as the Law of Moses not only prohibited any representation of the human form, but also regarded any object that had come into contact with a human corpse to be ritually unclean.

To avoid any scruple on the part of King Abgar, the Shroud was folded and decorated so that only the Holy Face of Jesus was visible. He welcomed the picture of Christ as he had yearned to see Jesus in person. King Abgar then beheld a vision emanating from the face of Addai that cured him of his leprosy. Addai then baptized Abgar and proceeded to lay the foundations of Christianity in Edessa, foundations so strong that Edessa would eventually become one of the first predominantly Christian cities in the world. Afterwards, Addai would depart Edessa (probably for Iran), leaving the picture of Christ with the King.

The Teaching of Addai and the historian Eusebius both state that "Addai" was one of the seventy-two chosen by Christ near the end of His public mission. Eusebius even gives his full name as Thaddaeus.[1] St Jerome, however, writing later identifies Addai as the Apostle Jude Thaddaeus.[2] Despite this confusion, and the ridicule of modern critics, the following supports the likelihood of an Apostolic mission with the Shroud to Edessa:

1. A mission to a King would more likely have been entrusted to an Apostle;
2. The traditional date of the mission coincides with the dispersion of the Apostles;
3. Traditions concerning St Jude Thaddaeus all state that he undertook missionary work in Mesopotamia, which includes Edessa, and was later martyred in Iran;
4. Edessan church history knows of no burial site for their founder, which is consistent with the tradition that St Jude moved on to Iran;
5. Traditional Christian art often depicts St Jude carrying an image of Christ;
6. Certain pollen samples taken from the Shroud of Turin are from a plant that grows only on the Anatolian plateau near Edessa;
7. The Shroud's connection with Edessa is historically certain, having been rediscovered after an earthquake in a hollow in one of the city gates in the sixth century, and then it was taken to Constantinople after the Moslems captured Edessa in the tenth century, and by Crusaders to France in the thirteenth century.

The Teaching of Addai goes on to relate that the Christian Faith thrived in Edessa both under Abgar the Black and his son Manu V until AD 57, when another son, Manu VI, became King and began a general persecution. This persecution caused the Shroud to be hidden and resulted in the almost total destruction of the Christian community. It was

---

[1] Eusebius, *The History of the Church*, 1:13.
[2] *Commentary on the Gospel of St Matthew* I, 10, 57 (AD 398).

to be nearly another one hundred and fifty years before a revival of Christianity would be initiated under Palut, the first Bishop of Edessa.

The Apostle Thomas, once the doubter, would become the dauntless. His allotted mission was India and her teeming millions living in the darkness of pantheistic negation. St Thomas made his way along the established overland trade route towards the city of Taxila in the Indus Valley (along the way, St Thomas may have preached Christ and established churches in Mesopotamia and Iran). Being formerly under Persian control, Taxila and its King, the Parthian Gundofarr, spoke Aramaic, which enabled St Thomas to preach the Gospel and have time to learn the local Indian language of Prakrit. There was probably also a Jewish colony in the same city, as was the case with most cities in the Roman and Parthian Empires.

St Thomas remained for several years in Taxila, making some converts there and throughout the Punjab. During these years, he also came to learn about the gods Shiva and Kali and the magnitude of the evil they represented. In AD 50, St Thomas returned to Jerusalem for Our Lady's Dormition and the Council of Jerusalem. The new Indian Church was left in the hands of a convert named Gaurasva. Soon afterwards, the Punjab was invaded by Kushan barbarians who swept away the Kingdom of Gundofarr and probably the small Christian community with it.

Hearing of the disaster in Taxila, St Thomas determined to restart his missionary efforts in more peaceful southern India. This time (AD 51), he would make his way by ship along the newly discovered monsoonal route across the Arabian Sea. Along the way, St Thomas stopped at the island of Socotra preaching the Gospel for about a year and making numerous converts. In 1542, St Francis Xavier would encounter the legacy of St Thomas' evangelism in the hills of that same island during his own epic journey to the Sub-continent.

During the monsoon sailing season of AD 52 St Thomas arrived in Cranganore, in the southern tip of India. All traditions state that he was alone. No other Apostle faced such a daunting challenge. Quickly learning the new language of Tamil, St Thomas proclaimed Christ and denounced the evil of Shiva. His success was significant, with thousands receiving baptism and hundreds being miraculously cured. St Thomas' work was epic, yet the only reliable records surviving come from his Indian opponents:

Their Keralolpattis tell how 'Thoman, an opponent of all vedas' came to the Malabar coast and converted 'many prominent people in the land.' The Nagargarandhravaryola of the family Kalathu Mana notes: 'Kali year 3153 (AD 52) the foreigner Thomas Sanyasi came to our village, preached there causing pollution. We therefore came away from that village.' This was in Palayur, where a Christian church stands to this day on the ruins of a Hindu temple. The tradition of the Jews who came to Cranganore in 68 is that a Christian community already existed there when they arrived.[3]

Nevertheless, the greatest proof of St Thomas' successful mission in India is the Church that currently exists to this day, a Church with sixty generations of Christians. St Pantaenus, founder of the Catechetical School in Alexandria, discovered Christians in India knowing of the Gospel of St Matthew before AD 200.[4] A bishop "of India and Persia" was present at the Council of Nicaea in AD 325. Cosmos Indicopleustes in his *Topographia* writes of Indian Christian communities with their own bishop c. AD 535. When the Portuguese arrived in 1498 they found that the Indian Christians called themselves "the Nazrani" (or, the Nazarenes), the first designation for believers in Christ.

After seventeen years, St Thomas decided to travel to the other side of the Indian peninsula and preach on the Coromandel coast. He came eventually to Mylapore, near the city of Madras. St Thomas again challenged the supremacy of Kali, to the hatred of the local Brahmin. One day in AD 72, while praying in a cave on Little Mount hill, St Thomas was attacked by some Brahmin, one of them piercing the Apostle through the heart with a lance. He was buried in Mylapore, where Indian Christians have ever since venerated his tomb.[5]

Forty-two years earlier, St Thomas had said, "Let us also go, that we may die like him" (John 11:16). By traveling to India, St Thomas had certainly gone a long way for his Master, and by a lance through the heart, died like Him.

---

[3] Warren H. Carroll, *The Founding of Christendom*, ibid., p. 418.
[4] Eusebius, *The History of the Church*, 5:10.
[5] St Gregory of Tours in the sixth century was acquainted with a pilgrim to St Thomas' tomb; and recent dating has established that the bricks used to construct the original tomb were of first century manufacture.

Themes for study:
- The work of St Jude Thaddaeus in Edessa.
- The early history of the Shroud of Turin.
- St Thomas' first mission in northern India.
- St Thomas' second mission in southern India.

Further reading:
- *The Catholic Encyclopaedia* (1911, vol. XIV, pp. 678-684).
- Warren H. Carroll, *The Founding of Christendom* (A History of Christendom), Vol. 1, Christendom Press, 1985, pp. 408-410.
- Anne W. Carroll, *Christ the King: Lord of History*, Second Edition, Trinity Communications, 1986, p. 83.
- F. X. Funk, *A Manual of Church History*, Vol. 1, Burns Oates & Washbourne, 1931, pp. 34 & 37.

The Council of Jerusalem

By AD 50, most of the Apostles had been dispersed and working outside Judea and among Gentiles for nearly ten years: St Peter in Antioch and Rome; Sts Paul and Barnabas in Antioch, Cyprus and Asia Minor; St Jude in Edessa; and St Thomas in India. There were large numbers of Gentile converts, as well as important ones such as Pomponia Graecina and King Agbar. None of these converts were expected to comply with the ritual and ceremonial obligations of the Law of Moses or required to keep themselves separate from the Jewish members of the Church.

On returning to Antioch from their first missionary journey to Cyprus and Asia Minor, Sts Paul and Barnabas gathered the local church together and related "all that God had done with them, and how he had opened a door of faith to the Gentiles." But some zealots from Judea declared, "Unless you are circumcised according to the custom of Moses, you cannot be saved." These Judaizing zealots also claimed to have support in Jerusalem. Sts Paul and Barnabas entered debate with them, and afterwards they, together with "some of the others" were appointed to go up to Jerusalem to the Apostles and the elders to obtain an answer from them.

Arriving in Jerusalem, the delegation from Antioch was welcomed by the Church, the Apostles and the elders, and Sts Paul and Barnabas again declared all that God had done with them among the Gentiles. But some that belonged to the party of the Pharisees rose up and said, "It is necessary to circumcise them, and to charge them to keep the law of Moses" For had not Christ Himself observed the Law of Moses in full? It was then determined that the Apostles and elders gather together to resolve the question.

In the first phase of the 'Council of Jerusalem' there was "much debate" over the entry of Gentiles into the Church. Then St Peter stood up and spoke authoritatively on the issue: "Brethren, you know that in the early days God made choice among you, that by my mouth the Gentiles should hear the word of the gospel and believe. And God who knows the heart bore witness to them, giving them the Holy Spirit just as he did to us; and he made no distinction between us and them, but cleansed their hearts by faith. Now therefore why do you make trial of God by putting a yoke upon the neck of the disciples which neither our fathers nor we have been able to bear? But we believe that we shall be saved through the grace of the Lord Jesus, just as they will." Then there was silence as the multitude contemplated St Peter's words. Next, Sts Paul and Barnabas spoke relating "what signs and wonders God had done through them among the Gentiles." St James the Less, Bishop of Jerusalem and an Apostle with little or no contact with Gentile converts, then asked to be heard. The Judaizers might have hoped that he would oppose Sts Peter and Paul, but instead he echoed the words of St Peter, with an added provision: "Brethren, listen to me ... my judgment is that we should not trouble those of the Gentiles who turn to God, but should write to them to abstain from the pollutions of idols and from unchastity and from what is strangled and from blood." These last words were added having pastoral considerations in mind, in order to conciliate the extreme Judaizers who abhorred these things and ensure natural contact between the Gentile and Jewish Christians.

It is argued by some that St James' statement ("Brethren, listen to me") was an ecclesiastical dictate denoting supreme authority over the Council as he was bishop of Jerusalem. This is reinforced by his words, "Therefore my judgment is that we should not trouble those of the Gentiles who turn to God." The consequence of such an argument is that St James was the final and undisputed decision-maker and St Peter had no absolute authority at all.

Such a conclusion, however, is without warrant. The Greek for "listen to me" is *akousate*, which is not of itself an imperative connoting authority but rather a word that can be used by any person seeking the attention of another. It is used hundreds of times in the New Testament in this sense. As for the words "my judgment", the original Greek words are *ego krino*, which mean "I give my opinion, or voice." The fact that St James spoke in the first person singular ("me", "my" or "I") suggests in itself that he was only giving his opinion, conviction or recommendation, one that was in line with St Peter's earlier statement.

After the conclusion of debate, the Council drafted the following letter, to be delivered by Sts Paul and Barnabas, together with Barsabbas, and Silas, to the Church in Antioch: "The brethren, both the apostles and the elders, to the brethren who are of the Gentiles in Antioch and Syria and Cilicia, greeting. Since we have heard that some persons from us have troubled you with words, unsettling your minds, although we gave them no instructions, it has seemed good to us, having come to one accord, to choose men and send them to you with our beloved Barnabas and Paul, men who have risked their lives for the sake of our Lord Jesus Christ. We have therefore sent Judas and Silas, who themselves will tell you the same things by word of mouth. For it has seemed good to the Holy Spirit and to us to lay upon you no greater burden than these necessary things: that you abstain from what has been sacrificed to idols and from blood and from what is strangled and from unchastity. If you keep yourselves from these, you will do well. Farewell."

Though there was rejoicing in Antioch over the decision of the Council, not all were satisfied. Some of the Judaizers remained obstinate, continuing to insist on observance of the Law of Moses in full for all converts, Jews and non-Jews. They would foment discord and division as far away as Corinth and Galatia. Their controversies would cause St Paul to call them "false brethren", and later compel him to write his most vigorous of letters — his epistle to the Galatians: "I am astonished that you are so quickly deserting him who called you in the grace of Christ and turning to a different gospel — not that there is another gospel, but there are some who trouble you and want to pervert the gospel of Christ." In subsequent decades, these Judaizers would break completely with the Church, becoming a separate sect known to history as the Ebionites.

The Council of Jerusalem, on the other hand, goes down in history as the first great ecumenical council, setting the pattern after which the next twenty gatherings would be modeled. The whole event also shows that from Apostolic times the leaders of the Church (the Pope and the other bishops of the world united to him) have always existed and acted as a living teaching authority to determine, with the assistance of the Holy Spirit, vital questions relating to faith and morals: "*For it has seemed good to the Holy Spirit and to us* to lay upon you no greater burden than these necessary things"

Themes for study:
- The demand of the Judaizers that Gentile converts comply with the whole Law of Moses.
- The referral of the dispute to the Apostles and elders in Jerusalem.
- The proceedings of the Council of Jerusalem.
- The promulgation of the Council's decree and the continued resistance of the extreme Judaizers.

Further reading:
- *Acts of the Apostles*, chapter 15.
- *The Catholic Encyclopaedia* (1911, vol. VIII, pp. 537-538).
- Warren H. Carroll, *The Founding of Christendom* (A History of Christendom), Vol. 1, Christendom Press, 1985, pp. 413-415.
- Rev. D. I. Lanslots, *The Primitive Church*, TAN Books and Publishers, 1926, pp. 149-155.
- Fr John Laux, *Church History*, TAN Books and Publishers, 1930, pp. 18-20.

The Later Missions of Sts Peter and Paul

St Paul's third great missionary journey began once more from Antioch, in AD 53. He made his way directly westwards, through Tarsus, Iconium and across to Ephesus. St Paul settled in Ephesus for two years, teaching and preaching in the "hall of Tyrannus", laying the foundations for the Church in the most important metropolis of Asia. From Ephesus, St Paul also strengthened the Faith in many of the surrounding cities and sent St Timothy and Erastus to Macedonia, as well as three (or even perhaps four) epistles to the Corinthians.

St Paul's success in Ephesus was so great that "the name of the Lord Jesus was extolled" among both Greeks and Jews. Books on magic arts to the value of fifty thousand pieces of silver were brought by converts and burned in public. The silversmiths of the city, believing that the whole of Asia was turning away from the worship of Diana, feared for the imminent financial ruin of their idol-making businesses: "'And there is danger not only that this trade of ours may come into disrepute but also that the temple of the great goddess Artemis may count for nothing' ... When they heard this they were enraged, and cried out, 'Great is Artemis of the Ephesians!'" The ensuing riot lasted for two hours, after which St Paul decided to depart Ephesus for Greece. Revisiting the churches of Macedonia and Corinth, St Paul confirmed the brethren in the Faith.

While in Corinth, he wrote his masterpiece, the epistle to the Romans in late AD 57. In this epistle St Paul greets many in Rome, though he makes no mention of St Peter. Neither does St Paul mention St Peter in any letters written while detained in Rome during AD 61-62. St Peter had probably returned to the capital of the Empire from northern Asia Minor in AD 55, the year after Claudius' murder. There, he would remain for nearly three years, during which he ordained Linus and Cletus as bishops and commissioned St Mark to write his Gospel. Sometime during AD 57 (and before the composition of the epistle to the Romans), the Fisherman decided to return to Asia Minor to work again among the churches of Bithynia, Pontus and Cappadocia. This second missionary visit would be a long one, lasting five years. St Mark departed Rome with St Peter and, according to Eusebius, made his way to Alexandria in Egypt in AD 58. When St Peter decided to return to Rome in AD 62 he asked St Mark to return with him, leaving Alexandria in the hands of Anianus. Certainly, the two were together in Rome after AD 62, as evidenced by the greetings at the end of St Peter's first epistle.[1]

After writing his letter to the Romans, St Paul determined to journey back to Jerusalem. He hoped to be there by the Passover of AD 58, but due to the plots of the Jews had to go by a roundabout route, thus not arriving until Pentecost. After greeting St James, St Paul made his way to the Temple. There, he was spotted by "Jews from Asia" and was accused of introducing a Gentile into the most sacred place of Judaism. The Jews set upon him, and St Paul would certainly have been beaten to death had not Roman soldiers from the local garrison intervened.

From the protective custody of the Romans in the fortress of Antonia, St Paul was sent under heavy guard to Caesarea to be judged by the Governor, Felix. After hearing his spirited defense, the Governor decided to keep St Paul in open confinement, where he remained for two years (during which, the Governor hoped to receive a large bribe, but none was forthcoming; also, St Luke composed his Gospel). It was now-abouts that Christ once more appeared to St Paul, assuring him of his imminent release: "Take courage, for as you have testified about me at Jerusalem, so you must bear witness also at Rome." Before the next Governor, Festus, St Paul again defended himself, this time exercising his right as a Roman citizen to appeal to the Emperor in Rome (who at this time was Nero):"You have appealed to Caesar; to Caesar you shall go."

Embarking on a wheat ship sailing from Alexandria to Rome, the first part of the voyage was uneventful enough. However, after passing Crete the ship was caught in a violent storm near the Adriatic Sea and for more than two weeks drifted aimlessly. Many despaired for their lives, but St Paul received reassurance from an angel that no one would be lost: "Do not be afraid, Paul; you must stand before Caesar; and lo, God has granted you all those who sail with you." Eventually, the ship found itself upon the

---

[1] St Mark would return to Alexandria in AD 68, the year after St Peter's martyrdom in Rome. According to Egyptian tradition, the Evangelist was himself martyred in the same year, being dragged by rope along the stone streets of Alexandria by a wild mob of Serapis-worshippers.

shores of Malta. There, the crew and all the passengers remained for the winter, leaving for Italy in spring. Early in AD 61, St Paul arrived in Rome.

"...you must stand before Caesar." So did St Paul, though we know nothing of what he said or how Nero reacted. In most probability, St Paul was kept under house arrest for two years and then released for lack of evidence. The Jews apparently let the case go by default. Throughout, and with St Luke at his side (composing now the Acts of the Apostles), St Paul followed in the footsteps of the Fisherman and preached Jesus Christ in the capital of the Empire: "And he lived there two whole years at his own expense, and welcomed all who came to him, preaching the kingdom of God and teaching about the Lord Jesus Christ quite openly and unhindered" Details of these two years in Rome are found in the "Captivity Epistles" (Ephesians, Philippians, Colossians, Philemon), which were written by St Paul during this time.

By now (AD 62-63), St Peter was again back in Rome for his third and final sojourn. This sojourn would last five years and encompass the burning of Rome and the Neronian persecution, climaxing in his glorious martyrdom. Before these troubles, though, St Peter would compose his two canonical letters and work tirelessly with St Mark in the continued building of the Church. It was perhaps during AD 63 that St Paul fulfilled his desire to travel to Spain, though no record or tradition survives to provide any details. At the outbreak of the Neronian persecution we find him again in Rome, only to flee soon afterwards with St Luke to Greece.

Themes for study:
- St Paul's third missionary journey.
- St Peter's second missionary journey to Asia Minor.
- St Peter's second and third sojourns in Rome.
- St Paul's fourth journey to Rome, and perhaps to Spain.

Further reading:
- *Acts of the Apostles*, chapters 19-28.
- Eusebius, *The History of the Church*, Book II, 19-22.
- Warren H. Carroll, *The Founding of Christendom* (A History of Christendom), Vol. 1, Christendom Press, 1985, pp. 420-423.
- Rev. D. I. Lanslots, *The Primitive Church*, TAN Books and Publishers, 1926, pp. 166-222.

The Neronian Persecution

The Roman Empire had been relatively well governed during the time of the Emperor Claudius. In the thirteen years of his reign (AD 41-54) the Church enjoyed remarkable growth and relative peace. But these years were to come to an abrupt end through the machinations of Claudius' niece and wife, the incestuous Julia Agrippina.

Agrippina had been previously married to the sinister Domitius Ahenobarbus, and from him had one child, later renamed Tiberius Claudius Nero. Nero was five years younger than Claudius' own son from a previous marriage, Britannicus, but Agrippina was determined that Nero would succeed as Emperor. Her constant scheming soon came to the attention of Claudius, forcing Agrippina to act swiftly and murder her beloved husband with a dish of poisoned mushrooms. After having Nero proclaimed Emperor in October 54, Agrippina then poisoned Britannicus the following year.

Being only sixteen years old at the time of his ascension to the throne, Nero could not govern in his own right. In his stead, the philosopher Seneca and the Praetorian Prefect Burrus governed the Empire ably for the next five years. However, while Rome flourished during these years, Nero's pride and psychopathic megalomania was growing. In the spring of AD 59, he had his manipulative mother murdered, with the consent of Seneca and Burrus. He then divorced and murdered his wife Octavia and married his mistress Poppaea. Seneca and Burrus could still exercise some restraint over Nero, but when Burrus died Nero forced Seneca into retirement. In the place of Burrus, Nero appointed the vicious Tigellinus, a man who did not hesitate to execute any one Nero believed had criticized him. Unrestrained, Nero began to insist more and more on being publicly glorified for his imagined sporting and artistic talents: a thirty-eight meter statue of himself was erected in the Imperial Palace; enormous parties were held to celebrate his athletic 'victories'; and the Roman nobility were forced to attend his musical performances and praise his efforts.

Nero had hitherto been unconcerned about the Christians, dismissing them as just an aberrant Jewish sect. The critical moment for the Christians would come after the night of 18 July, AD 64. The fires begun on that night would blaze for nine days and destroy ten of the fourteen districts of the great city on the Tiber. It was rumored that Nero "fiddled while Rome burned", and that he had planned the fire in order to build a grander palace and city for himself named Neronia. The burnt-out mob began to blame their matricidal Emperor for the disaster, and Nero, desperate to direct their fury elsewhere, concocted the story that it was the already unpopular Christians who had ignited the fires as part of a plot to destroy the Empire:

> ... and yet the evil rumors that the fire had been lighted at his order, could not be hushed. Therefore, in order to put an end to this talk, he designated culprits and had them punished with the utmost refinements of cruelty. And the people he chose were those whom the populace abominated on account of their vices and whom they called 'Christians' ... Therefore those who confessed their religion were arrested first of all; then, on their indication, great numbers were convicted who were accused not so much of fire-raising as of hatred of the human race.[1]

Nero would go the full stride and enact the only law that survived his execrable reign – the banning of Christianity. It was now an offense punishable with death to be a believer in Jesus Christ anywhere in the Empire. Thus, began the first of ten great Roman persecutions of Christianity that would span the next 248 years. The first victims were the Christians of Rome, who were hunted down and rounded up for the games of AD 64 in Nero's Circus. The entertainment for the Roman populace would be novel and exciting enough to be the distraction needed by Nero: Christians as food for wild beasts in the arena; Christians soaked in pitch and sulfur and lit as torches along the Appian Way and for the Emperor's parties; Christians forced to act as characters murdered in plays; Christian women given as sexual prizes to the victors of gladiatorial contests and then murdered. Though the mob reveled in these spectacles,

---

[1] Tacitus, *Annals of Imperial Rome*, 15, 44:2-5.

the more noble Romans admired the constancy of the martyrs and remained suspicious of Nero's motives for targeting them.

The persecution spread to other parts of the Empire, particularly the Christian communities in Asia Minor founded by Sts Peter and Paul. St Peter, in Rome continually since AD 62 and himself the prime target of the persecution, wrote to strengthen and inspire his former flock in the face of the same "fiery ordeal" befalling them:

> Peter, an apostle of Jesus Christ, to the Exiles of the dispersion in Pontus, Galatia, Cappadocia, Asia, and Bithynia ...
> ... Beloved, do not be surprised at the fiery ordeal which comes upon you to prove you, as though something strange were happening to you. But rejoice in so far as you share Christ's sufferings, that you may also rejoice and be glad when his glory is revealed (1 Pet. 1:1; 4:12-13).

Everywhere, Nero's soldiers were on the hunt for the leaders of the hated Christians. Apostles and Evangelists were together caught in the storm. St Luke abruptly ended his composition of the *Acts of the Apostles* and accompanied St Paul to Greece. However, in AD 66, St Paul was arrested near Troy and brought in chains back to Rome, where he was kept in close confinement, abandoned and alone. Put on trial for his life, St Paul defended himself with his customary skill, extending his opponents to two court sessions before being given the appropriate punishment for a Roman citizen — death by beheading. The sentence was carried out three miles outside of Rome on the Ostian Way, near the present Church of St Paul's Outside the Walls, probably in the year AD 67 (according to St Jerome). Finally, the great Apostle of the Gentiles had received the reward he envisaged when writing earlier to his beloved disciple, St Timothy:

> I have fought the good fight, I have finished the race, I have kept the faith. Henceforth there is laid up for me the crown of righteousness, which the Lord, the righteous judge, will award to me on that Day, and not only to me but also to all who have loved his appearing (2 Tim. 4:7-8).

For St Peter, justice would be much more summary in nature. According to tradition, while fleeing Rome, Christ appeared to him carrying his Cross towards the Eternal City. Upon asking Christ where He was going (*"Quo vadis, Domine?"*), St Peter was told, "Back to Rome to be re-crucified." St Peter understood this to mean that he should return and suffer martyrdom for Christ together with the afflicted Christians in Rome. After being arrested, St Peter was condemned to die by crucifixion, but out of humility did not want to die as his Master did, and so asked to be crucified upside down. The Romans gladly obliged, setting the cross on Vatican Hill, in the gardens of Nero. He was buried at the foot of the hill, the date being 29 June, AD 67.[2]

St Peter died a glorious death, fulfilling the wonderful prophesy of Christ spoken to him decades earlier when he was still a young and insignificant Galilean:

> Truly, truly, I say to you, when you were young, you girded yourself and walked where you would; but when you are old, you will stretch out your hands, and another will gird you and carry you where you do not wish to go. (This he said to show by what death he was to glorify God.) And after this he said to him, "Follow me" (John 21:18-19).

The historic evidence testifying to St Peter's martyrdom in Rome is strong, and includes testimonies from the following Church Fathers:

(i) St Irenaeus of Lyons(c. AD 180) refers to the Church in Rome as "the greatest and most ancient Church known to all, founded and organized at Rome by the two most glorious Apostles, Peter and Paul" (*Against Heresies* 3,3,2);

(ii) Tertullian (AD 200) speaks of St Peter ordaining St Clement in Rome (*Demurrer Against the Heretics* 32) and of St Peter baptizing in the Tiber River (*On Baptism* 4);

(iii) Clement of Alexandria (Ante AD 217) speaks of St Peter proclaiming the word of God publicly in Rome (In Eusebius, *The History of the Church* 6, 14);

---

[2] It is of great significance that the bones declared to be those of St Peter by Pope Paul VI on 29 June, 1968, do not include any feet bones, leading to the hypothesis that the Romans severed his feet at the ankles when bringing him down from the cross.

(iv)   Caius (AD 214) referred to Pope Victor as thirteenth bishop of Rome after St Peter (In Eusebius, *The History of the Church* 5, 28);
(v)   St Hippolytus of Rome (AD 225) names St Peter as first bishop of Rome (*Dict. Christian Biog.*, I, 577);
(vi)   St Cyprian of Carthage (AD 250) speaks of the "the place of Peter" (*Ep. Ad Anton.*) and "the seat of Peter" (*Ep. ad Cornel.*);
(vii) Firmilian of Caesaria (257 AD) speaks of the "succession of Peter" and "the chair of Peter" (*Ep. ad Cyp.*);
(viii) The Council of Sardica (AD 342-343) "honors the memory of the Apostle Peter" by referring appeals to the See of Peter (*Can. IV* and *Ep. ad Julium*);
(ix)   Pope Julius I (AD 337-352) referred to the doctrines received by him as coming from St Peter (*Apud. Apol. Athanas.* 35);
(x)   St Athanasius (AD 358) called Rome the Apostolic Throne (*Hist. Arian. ad. Monach.*, 35);
(xi)   St Optatus of Milevis says that the episcopal chair in Rome was first established by St Peter, in which chair sat St Peter himself (*Schism. Donat.* II, 2);
(xii) Pope Damasus (AD 370) speaks of the "Apostolic Chair (in which the) holy Apostle sitting, taught his successors how to guide the helm of the Church" (*Ep. 9, ad Synod, Orient. Apud Theodoret,* V., 10);
(xiii) St Ambrose (AD 387-390) refers to "Peter's chair" where "Peter, first of the apostles, first sat" (*De Poenit.* I., 7-32, *Exp. Symb. Ad Initiand.*).[3]

After St Peter's martyrdom, the leadership of the Church passed to Linus, of whom we know very little. He had been a slave and was ordained by St Peter, and had attended St Paul in prison in his lonely last hours. As for his qualifications to be the successor to the Fisherman, we know only this: that St Peter had trusted him and St Paul loved him. That is enough.

As for Nero, his reign as Emperor would degenerate into greater debauchery, murder, and madness, to the point where even pagan Romans

---

[3] Herbert Cardinal Vaughan, Archbishop of Westminster, Tenth Lecture at Free Trade Hall, Manchester, England, Autumn 1895.

had had enough. The cry of revolt was raised across Gaul, Germany, Briton and Spain. The Senate declared him an outlaw and sentenced him to a commoner's death. The Praetorian Guard then switched its allegiance to General Galba. As a group of Praetorians pursued his chariot, Nero realized that his end had come, and so took his own life with a dagger. With his suicide, ended the persecution of the Church. Nero's last words were, "What an artist dies in me!"

Themes for study:
- Nero's pride and psychopathic megalomania.
- Nero's burning of Rome and his scapegoating of the Christians.
- The cruelty of the persecution inflicted on the Christians.
- The martyrdoms of Sts Peter and Paul.

Further reading:
- Warren H. Carroll, *The Founding of Christendom* (A History of Christendom), Vol. 1, Christendom Press, 1985, pp. 419-426.
- Anne W. Carroll, *Christ the King: Lord of History*, Second Edition, Trinity Communications, 1986, pp. 85-86.
- Fernard Hayward, *A History of the Popes*, J.M. Dent & Sons Ltd., 1931, pp. 13-15.

The Jewish Revolt AD 66-70

"And as some spoke of the temple, how it was adorned with noble stones and offerings, he said, 'As for these things which you see, the days will come when there shall not be left here one stone upon another that will not be thrown down.' And they asked him, 'Teacher, when will this be, and what will be the sign when this is about to take place?'" (Luke 21: 5-7).

The time for the fulfillment of these prophetic words would come while Nero was at the height of his madness and depravity. As Nero's exercise of power grew unchecked, he would appoint officers similar to himself in nature – cruel, greedy and foolish. Two such men were appointed successively as Procurators of Judea – Albinius and Florus. Their respective rules were sufficiently corrupt and unjust to drive the Jews, who for decades had been simmering with agitation, into open revolt.

The revolutionaries, who had hitherto been divided into competing factions, laid aside their quarrels to form a single force against the hated Romans – the Zealots (or *"Sicarii"* – "daggermen"). The majority of Pharisees, fearing a recurrence of Caligula's attempts to desecrate the Temple and inspired by Messianic hopes, joined the Zealots. Riots broke out in Caesarea and elsewhere against local Greeks and then in Jerusalem itself. The fortress stronghold of Masada with its store of arms was captured. The priest Eleazar then prevailed upon the High Priest to end public prayers for the Emperor in the Temple. This was the signal for universal revolt. By the end of August AD 66, the whole of Jerusalem was in the hands of the Zealots. The Roman garrison was induced to surrender under promise of safe passage from Judea. The promise was not kept, and the garrison was massacred.

In response, the Governor of Syria, Gallus, brought down the Twelfth Legion (*Fulminata* – the "Thundering One") to suppress the revolt. Marching down the coast, he successfully entered Jerusalem and besieged the Temple Mount, before a Jewish counter-attack drove the

Legion out of the city. Retreating through Beth-horon (the scene of great victories won by Joshua and Judas Maccabeus), the Romans were attacked. The Twelfth Legion was destroyed, its siege equipment captured and its eagle taken. Free from imminent Roman intervention, the Zealots set up government in Jerusalem, divided the country into seven military districts, and began minting their own silver coins.

When news reached Nero of the Twelfth Legion's defeat, he was in Greece engaging in his usual buffooneries and immorality. Nevertheless, he still possessed sufficient sense to appoint the best man available to deal with the crisis – Titus Flavius Vespasianus (aka Vespasian), a 57-year-old general who possessed in his character the best of old Rome. Vespasian was dispatched to Palestine with three legions.

Vespasian's tactic was to first retrieve all the lost territories outside Judea itself. One by one they fell to him: Perea, Lydia, Jamnia. Galilee, defended by the priest Josephus (later the great Jewish historian), was next conquered after a forty-seven day siege. Inhabitants of captured towns were either massacred or given as slaves to the soldiers. In the winter of AD 68 two separate Zealot armies under John of Gischala and the priest Eleazar stormed Jerusalem and massacred everyone suspected of Roman sympathies. In all, eight thousand five hundred were killed, their blood forming a lake outside the Temple. This was the moment when the Jerusalem Christians under their new Bishop Simeon (who was perhaps the brother of St James the Less) fled to Pella beyond the Jordan. No doubt, they had remembered the prophesy of Jesus, spoken when weeping over Jerusalem:

> For the days shall come upon you, when your enemies will cast up a bank about you and surround you, and hem you in on every side, and dash you to the ground, you and your children within you, and they will not leave one stone upon another in you; because you did not know the time of your visitation (Luke 19: 43-44).

Meanwhile in Rome, leadership passed from one new Emperor to another in quick succession. After Nero's whimpering suicide in June AD 68, Galba, Otho and Vitellius all met premature deaths. There was almost as much chaos in Rome as there was in Jerusalem. In July AD 69, Vespasian's legions proclaimed him Emperor, followed by the Danubian legions a month later. Vespasian turned the Judean war over to his son, Titus, and marched on Rome, taking it in December AD 69.

Back in Judea, the situation was becoming desperate. The whole country was now subdued by the Romans except for Jerusalem. Division racked the Jewish leadership as forces loyal to either John of Gischala, the priest Eleazar and Simon bar Giora fought each other for control of the city, committing rapes and murders. Titus tightened his grip, moving up his legions for a full assault. The first attacks repulsed, Titus then determined to build a wall of circumvallation around the city, just as Christ had foretold. The siege would last five months. Catapults and battering rams pounded the city walls. No one could escape. Starvation began to grip the population of nearly a million people (a population swollen by Passover pilgrims). Men were eating leather and hay, mothers even their babies. The dead were piled up in rotting heaps and then thrown into the surrounding ravines:

> The Jews, unable now to leave the city, were deprived of all hope of survival. The famine became more intense and devoured whole houses and families. The roofs were covered with women and babes, the streets full of old men already dead. Young men and boys, swollen with hunger, haunted the squares like ghosts and fell wherever faintness overcame them. To bury their kinsfolk was beyond the strength of the sick ... many while burying others fell dead themselves, and many set out for their graves before their hour struck. In their misery no weeping or lamentation was heard; hunger stifled emotion ... Deep silence enfolded the city, and a darkness burdened with death ... Everyone as he breathed his last fixed his eyes on the Temple, turning his back on the partisans he was leaving alive ... (the dead were thrown) from the walls into the valleys. When in the course of his rounds Titus saw these choked with dead, and a putrid stream tricking from under the decomposing bodies, he groaned, and uplifting his hands called God to witness that this was not his doing.[1]

Titus offered generous surrender terms, but the Zealots refused to consider. On 9 August, AD 70, Titus personally led what would be the last assault. Breaching the city walls, the Roman troops engaged the defenders

---

[1] Josephus, *The Jewish War*, Penguin Classics, 1959, pp. 297-298.

in fierce hand-to-hand combat through the streets. By the end of the day, most of Jerusalem was in Roman hands, including the Outer Court of the Temple Precinct. The next morning, the battle was resumed for the Inner Court. Titus gave the specific order that the Temple was not to be destroyed, however, through the Golden Window of the Holies an angry Roman legionary threw a firebrand, causing the Sanctuary to blaze up. Titus desperately tried to put out the fire, but the surrounding soldiers ignored his efforts (and even orders) and threw more firebrands over his shoulder. The Temple burned to its bare stones. It was 10 August, the same day the Babylonians had destroyed the first Temple in 586 BC.

Titus now had no mercy for anything or anyone in Jerusalem. He ordered the Temple stones and the entire city raised: "they will not leave one stone upon another." All that now remains are the stones of the western retaining wall, known today as the Wailing Wall. Wanton killing and looting prevailed. No Jew was permitted anymore to live in Jerusalem — it would be the home of Caesar's Tenth Legion. The survivors, numbering ninety-seven thousand, were either taken to the arenas or enslaved to work at the service of Rome. Simon bar Giora and John of Gischala were taken to Rome and paraded through the streets in victory procession, together with the symbol of Judaism — the seven stick menorah — and other Temple treasures.

The scepter had now passed from Judea. AD 71 was the first year of a new world: one without Jerusalem, without the Temple, without the sacrifices. There would be no more kings, no more prophets, and no restoration. The Church was unaffected by the Jewish Revolt, and it now stood vindicated and reassured against those who had formerly mocked Christ and His prophesies. But it was still only a small, rag-tag band of believers, scattered across the triumphant Empire of steel, an Empire that still held them to be illegal.

Themes for study:
- The success of the initial stages of the Zealot revolt.
- The campaign and siege of Judea/Jerusalem by Vespasian/Titus.
- The destruction of the second Temple.
- The fulfillment of Christ's prophecy.

Further reading:
- Warren H. Carroll, *The Founding of Christendom* (A History of Christendom), Vol. 1, Christendom Press, 1985, pp. 425-429.
- Anne W. Carroll, *Christ the King: Lord of History*, Second Edition, Trinity Communications, 1986, pp. 86-87.
- Y. Aharoni and M. Avi-Yonah, *The Modern Bible Atlas*, Revised Ed., Allen and Unwin, 1977, pp. 247-248.

The Church in the Late First Century AD

During the years following the calamities of the Neronian persecution and the Jewish revolt, Christianity and the Church fade quietly to the background. The anti-Christian laws remained, yet between AD 70 and 90 not a single martyrdom is recorded. The seed had been planted, and was continuing to quietly spread its roots throughout all levels of society.

Pope Linus ruled the Church as the first successor to St Peter for nine years between AD 67 and 76. Very little is known of his life and pontificate, and what has come down is mostly apocryphal. Some conjecture that he was the same Linus mentioned by St Paul in 2 Timothy 4:21, but definite proof is lacking. The *Liber Pontificalis* (without identifying the source) states that he was a slave from Tuscany and his father's name was Herculanus. The same work also asserts that he issued a decree on women's dress and suffered martyrdom, both highly unlikely. There is some possibility that he was buried next to St Peter on Vatican Hill.

Pope Cletus, second successor to St Peter, governed the Church from AD 76 to 88. Details of his life are also scanty and unreliable. He was likewise a slave and his original name was Anencletus (meaning "blameless"; Cletus = "the called one"). The *Liber Pontificalis* tells us that his father's name was Emelianus and was a Roman by birth. It also tells us that he performed more than two-dozen ordinations and, like St Linus, was buried on Vatican Hill.

During the reigns of Sts Linus and Cletus, the Church made considerable progress, especially in Asia Minor. This was in large part due to the prevailing atmosphere of peace and tolerance of the Flavian emperors – Vespasian and his sons Titus and Domitian. Why such tolerance? Most probably, due to the number of Christians and Christian sympathizers within the Flavian family. The details are conjectural, but there is evidence that the following Flavians were Christians:

(i) Titus Flavius Sabinus, older brother of Vespasian and Prefect of Rome in AD 64. He was converted to Christianity by his wife, "St Petronilla";

(ii) St Petronilla, possibly the daughter of Pomponia Graecina, convert of St Peter. The Roman martyrology calls St Petronilla, "St Peter's daughter";

(iii) Flavius Clemens, son of Titus Flavius Sabinus, and nephew to the Emperor Vespasian. Consul for AD 95;

(iv) Flavia Domitilla, granddaughter of Vespasian and wife of Flavius Clemens;

(v) The children of Flavius Clemens and Flavia Domitilla, who were both Christians, and at the ages of six and five respectively were declared successors to the childless Domitian in AD 90;

(vi) Clement, slave of the household of Flavius Clemens, and future Pope;

(vii) Acilius Glabrio and his family. Acilius was Consul for AD 91. His family were certainly Christian;

(viii) M. Arrecinus Clemens, a relative of Flavius Clemens and Consul for AD 93;

(ix) Titus Flavius Sabinus III, son of Titus Flavius Sabinus, brother of Flavius Clemens and the husband of Domitian's niece.

It seemed that within less than two generations after the resurrection of Christ, the Roman Empire was on the verge of having a Christian Emperor. How the history of the world would have been different! But it was to be an aborted dream. After nine years of reasonable rule, a sudden and ugly change came over the Emperor Domitian around the year AD 90. To pay for his extravagances, Domitian extended the tax paid by the Jews to "all who lived like Jews", and began a search for religious innovators and "atheists." He also began to call himself *Dominus et Deus* ("Lord and God") and demand the same from others. Naturally, when the Christians around him refused to comply, Domitian moved against them. One after another, Christian members of his family, even those appointed to the annual consulate, were eliminated: Acilius Glabrio, M. Arrecinus Clemens, Titus Flavius Sabinus III and Flavius Clemens were all executed in AD 91, 93, 94 and 95 respectively. The wife of Flavius Clemens, Flavia Domitilla, was exiled to the rocky island of Pandataria.

Charges included "novelties", "atheism", "Jewish practices" and "disrespect towards Roman institutions."

Domitian's persecution spread beyond his family. The Christians of Asia Minor were particularly targeted. Many Christians in Pergamum were beheaded. Pliny the Younger, writing to the Emperor Trajan in AD 111, mentioned how Christians in the province of Bithynia had been forced to renounce their faith twenty years earlier. The last surviving Apostle, St John, was arrested and brought to Rome, and after miraculously escaping martyrdom in a cauldron of boiling oil, found himself exiled to the island of Patmos. Titus, bishop of Crete, and St Timothy, bishop of Ephesus, were respectively martyred in AD 96 and 97.

The last year of Domitian's reign resembled that of Nero's. He was now half-mad, and feared everything and everyone around him (it is said that he spent most of his time in a room of polished surfaces so he could see anyone attempting to attack him from behind). A reign of terror operated through a network of informers. All philosophers were driven from Italy and all citizens were compelled to swear by and sacrifice to his divine genius. In AD 96, a conspiracy of praetorians and palace officials ended the nightmare, sending a former slave of Flavius Clemens by the name of Stephanos to strike Domitian down with a dagger. The elderly and virtuous senator Nerva was named Emperor in his place. It is not known what ever happened to the two young Christian heirs to Domitian's throne.

Under Nerva, peace would return to the Church. The bishop of Rome at the time was St Clement, third successor to St Peter and Pope since AD 88. Of the life and death of St Clement very little is known. He had been a slave of Flavius Clemens and took the name of Clement in honor of his former master. St Irenaeus[1] states that St Clement knew and worshipped with Sts Peter and Paul. According to Tertullian[2], it was St Peter who ordained him as presbyter and then bishop. Both Origen and Eusebius identify him as the Clement who collaborated with St Paul and mentioned in his Epistle to the Philippians (4:3), but all other authorities doubt this. Around the AD 100, the Emperor Trajan had him exiled to the Chersonese (Crimea). There, he found two thousand other Christians,

---

[1] *Against Heresies* 3, 3, c. AD 180.
[2] *The Demurrer Against the Heretics* 32, c. AD 199.

also exiled and working in the marble quarries. They enjoyed a certain liberty that enabled St Clement to preach. Converts were numerous and churches were built. News reached Trajan, who ordered St Clement to sacrifice to the gods. Refusing, he was thrown into the Black Sea with an iron anchor around his neck.[3]

It was about AD 96-98 when Pope Clement wrote an epistle attempting to heal the ruptures in the Church of Corinth sparked by an insurrection against the bishop and presbyters that resulted in their deposition. This epistle was accorded an authority in the early Church second only to Scripture itself. As Eusebius writes:

> Clement has left us one recognized epistle, long and wonderful, which he composed in the name of the church of Rome ... in many churches this epistle was read aloud to the assembled worshippers in early days, as it is in our own.[4]

From the point of view of Church history, patrology and apologetics, St Clement's letter is of enormous significance, particularly as the better element of the Corinthians sought a remedy for their ills not from St John who was then still alive, but from the successor in Peter's Chair:

The primacy and universal jurisdiction of the Bishop of Rome:

> The Church of God which sojourns in Rome to the Church of God which sojourns in Corinth ... Owing to the sudden and repeated calamities and misfortunes which have befallen us, we must acknowledge that we have been somewhat tardy in turning our attention to the matters in dispute among you (Address 1:1).

---

[3] Around the year 868, St Cyril, while in the Crimea to evangelize the Kazars, dug up some bones in a mound together with an anchor and had them translated to Rome, whereupon they were deposited by Pope Adrian II in the high altar of the basilica of St Clement.
[4] Eusebius, *The History of the Church* 3, 4, 80.

Apostolic succession:

> The Apostles received the gospel for us from the Lord Jesus Christ; and Jesus Christ was sent from God. Christ, therefore, is from God, and the Apostles are from Christ. Both of these orderly arrangements, then, are by God's will. Receiving their instructions and being full of confidence on account of the resurrection of Our Lord Jesus Christ, and confirmed in faith by the word of God, they went forth in the complete assurance of the Holy Spirit, preaching the good news that the Kingdom of God is coming. Through countryside and city they preached; and they appointed their earliest converts, testing them by the spirit, to be the bishops and deacons of future believers. Nor was this a novelty: for bishops and deacons had been written about a long time earlier. Indeed, Scripture somewhere says: 'I will set up their bishops in righteousness and their deacons in faith' (42:1);
>
> Our Apostles knew through our Lord Jesus Christ that there would be strife for the office of bishop. For this reason, therefore, having received perfect foreknowledge, they appointed those who have already been mentioned, and afterwards added the further provision that, if they should die, other approved men should succeed to their ministry ... (44:1-5).

The office of Bishop and Priest, their authority and their sacrifices:

> He has commanded the offerings and services to be celebrated, and not carelessly nor in disorder, but at fixed times and hours ... Those, then, who make their offerings at the appointed times, are acceptable and blessed; for they follow the laws of the Master and do not sin. To the high priest, indeed, proper ministrations are allotted, to the priests a proper place is appointed, and upon the levites their proper services are imposed. The layman is bound by the ordinances for the laity (40:1-5);
>
> Our sin will not be small if we eject from the episcopate those who blamelessly and holily have offered its Sacrifices. Blessed are those presbyters who have already finished their course, and who have obtained a fruitful and perfect release (44:5).

Early Church History

The Pope as the Vicar of Christ:

> Accept our counsel, and you will have nothing to regret. For as God lives, and as the Lord Jesus Christ lives, and the Holy Spirit, and the faith and hope of the elect, as surely will he that humbly and with equanimity and without regret carries out the commandments and precepts given by God, be enrolled and chosen among the number of those who are being saved through Jesus Christ, through whom there is glory to Him forever and ever. Amen (58:2).
>
> If anyone disobey the things which have been said by Him (Christ) through us, let them know that they will involve themselves in transgression and in no small danger (59:1).

Themes for study:
- The pontificates of Sts Linus and Cletus.
- The Flavian Christians.
- The Domitian persecution.
- The pontificate and epistle of St Clement.

Further reading:
- Warren H. Carroll, *The Founding of Christendom* (A History of Christendom), Vol. 1, Christendom Press, 1985, pp. 447-451.
- Eusebius, *The History of the Church*, Penguin Classics, 1989, Book III, 13-20.
- Fernard Hayward, *A History of the Popes*, J.M. Dent & Sons Ltd., 1931, pp. 18-20.

St John the Apostle

St John was the son of Zebedee, a pious and successful fisherman from the village of Bethsaida on the shore of Lake Genesareth in Galilee, some time about AD 10. His mother was Salome, who may have been a sister of Mary the Mother of Jesus, and one of the holy women who attended the daily needs of Christ and the Apostles. His older brother was James, who was also chosen by Christ and became the Apostle James the Greater. Like their father, John and James were both fishermen.

St John was originally a disciple of St John the Baptist, and together with St Andrew were the first of the Apostles chosen by Christ. With Sts Peter and James, St John was one of the favorite Apostles of the Lord; indeed, he was "the disciple whom Jesus loved." Tradition depicts St John as possessing a gentle character; however, Christ calls him and his brother the name *Boanerges*, "Sons of Thunder", implying rather an enthusiastic and impetuous character. St Paul numbers him, together with Sts Peter and James the Less, among the pillars of the Church (Gal. 2:9).

St John is mentioned in the Scriptures more times than any other Apostle, except St Peter.[1] He is with Our Lord at the raising of Jairus' daughter, at the Transfiguration, and at the agony in the Garden. Only he and St Peter were sent into Jerusalem to make preparation for the Last Supper. At the Supper itself, he reclines his head on Christ's breast. He courageously follows his Master with St Peter to the palace of Annas and Caiaphas, then to the Praetorium of Pilate, and is the only Apostle to go all the way to the foot of the Cross. Here, St John receives Christ's last will: "Woman, behold your son!"; "Behold, your Mother!"

After the resurrection of Christ, St John associates mostly with St Peter. It is they who together first run to the empty tomb and "believe"; they are together fishing on the Sea of Galilee when Christ appears to them from the shore; together they confront the Sanhedrin and defy their threats, enduring scourging and imprisonment; and together they work confirming the converts of Philip in Samaria. They probably parted in AD 42 after St Peter's decision to travel to Rome. Undoubtedly, they were briefly reunited again for the Council of Jerusalem in AD 49.

---

[1] St John is mentioned 29 times; St Peter 195 times.

The subsequent long history of St John's life is shrouded in silence and mystery. Tradition only provides small insights. Some suggest that he stayed with the Blessed Virgin Mary until her death in Jerusalem; others believe they traveled together to Asia and for some time lived in Ephesus[2], before returning to Jerusalem. After the Blessed Mother's dormition and assumption into heaven, St John probably went back to Asia Minor and spent most of his years in and about Ephesus, working with successive bishops to strengthen the churches there.

During the persecution of the Emperor Domitian, St John was arrested and thrown into a cauldron of boiling oil, only to be miraculously preserved like the three children in the Babylonian furnace (Dan. 3). According to Tertullian, this occurred in Rome at the Latin Gate. In frustration, Domitian exiled him to the island of Patmos in the Aegean Sea "on account of the word of God and the testimony of Jesus." There, he worked among the local inhabitants making many conversions. He also received the famous *Revelation*, prophesies directly from Christ designed to rekindle the original fervor and virtue of the Asian churches and strengthen them in the certainly of the triumph of good over evil. These prophesies will come to pass, but exactly how and when no one can tell. After the death of Domitian, the new Emperor, Nerva, recalled all exiles, allowing St John to return to Ephesus in AD 97. There, St John settled down to write his gospel and canonical letters. He did not assume the office as bishop of Ephesus[3], rather, as the last of the Apostles he held a unique status and authority. In his second and third epistles he simply calls himself "the elder." Many stories relate his constant exhortations to love one another: "My little children, love one another." He made himself the humblest of men and the servant of all, and even in his extreme old age would continue to work, pray, fast and travel for the sake of Christ and His Church. Much of his legacy would be passed on by two future giants of the second century Church who personally knew and conversed with him, Sts Ignatius of Antioch and Polycarp of Smyrna.

---

[2] The alleged 'House of Mary' in what was formerly Ephesus in modern-day Turkey has been a popular pilgrimage destination for Christians and even Moslems since the late nineteenth century.

[3] St Timothy had been the bishop of Ephesus immediately prior to St John's return, suffering martyrdom in AD 97. He was replaced by Onesimus, Philemon's runaway slave mentioned in St Paul's small epistle (Phile. 1:10).

St John did not write his gospel simply to provide another account of Christ's life and teachings. These were readily available through the circulation of the Synoptics. He wrote to meet the challenge of new philosophical heresies and errors denying that Jesus Christ was God incarnate, and that He possessed a real human nature while remaining the eternal Son of God. He considered this denial to be of the Antichrist: "For many deceivers have gone out into the world, men who will not acknowledge the coming of Jesus Christ in the flesh; such a one is the deceiver and the antichrist" (2 John 1:7). The chief propagator of such errors was Cerinthus, a circumcized Jew possessing a mixture of Jewish, Christian and Gnostic beliefs. St John abhorred his teachings with the utmost passion. One day he saw him in the baths of Ephesus, and rushed out exclaiming: "Let us fly, lest even the bath-house fall down, because Cerinthus, the enemy of truth is within." The sublimity of St John's gospel has caused him to be represented as an eagle, for he rose higher than any other of the sacred writers.

With the death of St John around the year AD 100 ended the apostolic age. A number of ancient writers held the belief that St John did not die, but like Henoch and Elias, was translated to an earthly paradise from where he would return to preach against the Antichrist. In this paradise he has the special privilege of seeing and enjoying God. This conclusion is based on Our Lord's words to St Peter: "If it is my will that he remain until I come, what is that to you? Follow me!" (John 21:22). The majority of other writers, however, admit that St John is dead and now reigns with Christ and all the other saints in heaven.

Themes for study:
- St John's status as one of the principal Apostles.
- St John's work in Ephesus and Asia Minor.
- St John's exile and his writing down of the *Book of Revelation*.
- St John's purpose for, and writing of, the fourth Gospel.

Further reading:
- *The Catholic Encyclopaedia* (1911, vol. VIII, pp. 492-493).
- Warren H. Carroll, *The Founding of Christendom* (A History of Christendom), Vol. 1, Christendom Press, 1985, pp. 451-453.
- Fr John Laux, *Introduction to the Bible*, TAN Books and Publishers, 1932, pp. 245-248.
- Mons. William L. Newton, *A Commentary on the New Testament*, The Catholic Biblical Association, 1942, pp. 293-295.

AD 101 to AD 200: THE APOSTOLIC FATHERS AND APOLOGISTS

Sts Ignatius of Antioch and Polycarp of Smyrna

After the Apostles themselves, there are few other names more famous in the early Church than those of Sts Ignatius of Antioch and Polycarp of Smyrna. Yet, we know virtually nothing about their respective origins and early lives. The little that we do know is gathered from their various epistles, written for the spiritual benefit of their flocks in Asia Minor, or from brief references gathered from other writings composed after their martyrdoms.

There was a pious tradition that St Ignatius was the child in the Scriptures brought to Christ and eulogized by Him as possessing those innocent qualities necessary for anyone who wishes to enter the Kingdom of Heaven. This tradition was based on St Ignatius' second name, Theophorus, meaning "bearing God", however, in most probability it is nothing more than myth. Nevertheless, his seven epistles do tell us that St Ignatius was worthy of the name Theophorus, bearing God in an heroic soul, in his hatred of heresy and schism, in his care for the unity of the Church, and in his great yearning for martyrdom.

Other sources tell us some details of the ecclesiastical career of St Ignatius. He was certainly a convert, and describes himself, like St Paul, as "one born out of time." He was the second successor to the See of Antioch in Syria after Sts Peter and Evodius. According to Eusebius, he was elevated to this see in the year AD 69.[1] It is highly possible that in his earlier years St Ignatius knew and worshipped with Sts Peter and Paul, as both spent considerable time in Antioch. Another tradition holds that it was St Peter himself who ordained St Ignatius a bishop: "... he obtained this office from those saints, and that the hands of the blessed apostles touched his sacred head."[2]

The immediate decades following the Neronian persecution (AD 64–67) were generally good years for the Church, with freedom from persecution allowing for extensive growth. During these decades, St Ignatius became a disciple of the Apostle John and good friends with St Polycarp of Smyrna. The Church was growing and spreading throughout the Roman world. It was now more distinctly gentile, and clearly a federation of communities united in belief, mode of government and worship.

However, around the year AD 115 the Imperial political mood again turned against Christianity and another persecution was launched, this time by the Emperor Trajan. An earthquake struck the city of Antioch while Trajan was sojourning there after his victorious conquest of Armenia and northern Mesopotamia. Thousands were killed, including one of the Consuls for that year. The Emperor himself was injured. Christians were blamed for the disaster and many were formally denounced and arrested. One of the first victims of the scapegoating was the city's bishop, St Ignatius.

St Ignatius, by now an elderly man, was "at least thirty years a bishop, probably trained by the Apostle John, and was apparently at this time the most venerated living member of the whole Church."[3] He was chained by the Romans and ordered by Trajan to be taken to Rome. There is no other case recorded in Church history of a Christian being so transported across the Empire for martyrdom. He was marched through Asia Minor to be eaten alive by lions in the Colosseum: "I am His wheat, ground fine by the lion's teeth to be made purest bread for Christ" (*Epistle*

---

[1] *The History of the Church* 3, 36.
[2] St John Chrysostom, *Homilies on St Ignatius and St Babylas*, in Schaff, Nicene and Post-Nicene Fathers, Ist Series, 9:136.
[3] Warren H. Carroll, *The Founding of Christendom*, Ibid., p. 455. Virtually nothing is known of the Popes during these years – Evaristus, Alexander I, and Sixtus I – besides their names, nationality and years of office.

to the Romans 4). Along the way, he was greeted by delegations from the various churches that flocked to venerate the renowned spiritual father.

It was during his dramatic journey to Rome that St Ignatius composed his now famous seven epistles in Greek addressed to the Christian communities of Ephesus, Magnesia, Tralles, Rome, Philadelphia, Smyrna and a personal one to St Polycarp. They were all probably written during two or three weeks in the summer of AD 116. These were letters of encouragement, edification and gratitude to those who had given him assistance. The principal themes emerging from his epistles include the authority of the clergy, the Eucharist as the real flesh of Christ, the hatred of heresy and division (Docetism and the Judaizers) and the greatness of martyrdom. In these epistles is also found the first use of the term "Catholic Church":

> "I am writing to all the Churches and I enjoin all, that I am dying willingly for God's sake, if only you do not prevent it. I beg of you, do not do me an untimely kindness. Allow me to be eaten by the beasts, which are my way of reaching to God" (*Letter to the Romans* 4:1).

> "It is necessary, therefore, – and such is your practice – that you do nothing without the bishop, and that you be subject also to the presbytery, as to the Apostles of Jesus Christ our hope, in whom we shall be found, if we live in Him. It is necessary also that the deacons, the dispensers of the mysteries of Jesus Christ, be in every way pleasing to all men. For they are not the deacons of food and drink, but servants of the Church of God ..." (*Letter to the Trallians* 2:2).

> "Take care, then, to use one Eucharist, so that whatever you do, you do according to God: for there is one Flesh of Our Lord Jesus Christ, and one cup in the union of His Blood; one altar, as there is one bishop with the presbytery and my fellow servants, the deacons" (*Letter to the Philadelphians* 4:1).

> "I did my best as a man devoted to unity. But where there is division and anger, God does not dwell. The Lord, however, forgives all who repent, if their repentance leads to the unity of God and to the council of the bishop. I have faith in the grace of

Jesus Christ; and He will remove from you every chain" (*ibid.* 8, 1).

"They abstain from the Eucharist and from prayer, because they do not confess that the Eucharist is the Flesh of our Savior Jesus Christ, Flesh which suffered for our sins and which the Father, in His goodness, raised up again. They who deny the gift of God are perishing in their disputes" (*Letter to the Smyrnaeans* 7:1).

"You must all follow the bishop as Jesus Christ follows the Father, and the presbytery as you would the Apostles. Reverence the deacons as you would the command of God. Let no one do anything of concern to the Church without the bishop. Let that be considered a valid Eucharist which is celebrated by the bishop, or by one whom he appoints. Wherever the bishop appears, let the people be there; just as wherever Jesus Christ is, there is the Catholic Church. Nor is it permitted without the bishop either to baptize or to celebrate the agape ..." (*ibid.* 8:1).

Due to St Ignatius' direct association with the Apostles themselves his writings are an invaluable testimony to the faith and practice of the Apostolic and immediate post-Apostolic Church. Up until the fifteenth century, fifteen epistles were attributed to St Ignatius including ones addressed to the Virgin Mary and St John. However, later, eight of these were recognized as spurious. The authenticity of the remaining seven Ignatian epistles was also long challenged by Protestants due to their clear presentation of an hierarchical and monarchical Church. Three versions of these seven epistles circulated, known respectively as the long, short and mixed recensions. The authenticity of the mixed recension has now been acknowledged by both Catholic and Protestant scholars including Lightfoot, Harnack, Zahn and Funk.

There exists no reliable eyewitness account of the actual death of St Ignatius in Rome. Undoubtedly, he lived up to his words in his epistle to the Romans. One tradition states that the final scene took place on 19 December in the Flavian Ampitheatre, that the death was probably the work of one moment, and afterwards his bones were collected by his friends and returned to Antioch.

Like St Ignatius of Antioch, St Polycarp of Smyrna was also a disciple of St John the Apostle and was conversant with many who had beheld Christ: "He was instructed by Apostles, and had had familiar intercourse with many who had seen Christ."[3] At eighty-five years of age he could still vividly remember St John's personal accounts of Christ's miracles and teaching and relate them on to his own disciples. This is the same Polycarp to whom St Ignatius addressed one of his epistles. St Polycarp's long life links the teachers and theologians of the mid-second century to the Apostolic founders of the Church.

We know some details of the life of St Polycarp through his pupil St Irenaeus of Lyons. St Polycarp was born of Christian parents and hence was a believer in Christ from his childhood: "Eighty-six years I have served him, and He has never done me wrong" (*The Martyrdom of St Polycarp* 9:3). He was considered a father figure in the Church of Asia Minor by Christians and pagans alike. Tertullian states that it was St John who appointed him to the see of Smyrna.[4]

Late in AD 154, St Polycarp visited Rome with St Irenaeus and met Pope St Anicetus to discuss their differences regarding the time for observing Easter. For Polycarp, the practice of St John celebrating the crucifixion and resurrection of Christ together and always on the 14th of Nisan was sacrosanct. The Pope disagreed but did not insist on conformity to the Roman practice, and both parted amicably after co-celebrating Mass at the first shrine built over the tomb of St Peter. Also while in Rome, St Polycarp preached vigorously against the Gnostics and Marcionites, bringing many back to the Church.

St Polycarp would not live long after returning from Rome. The League Festival of February AD 155 in honor of the Emperor ignited anti-Christian outbursts and a demand for Christian blood from both pagan and Jewish inhabitants. After ten Christians had been arrested, tortured and fed to the lions, the mob began crying out for the bishop's arrest. At the urging of his beloved followers, St Polycarp quit Smyrna. The Roman authorities pursued him relentlessly and tracked him down, finding him in the house of a friend deep in prayer for the Church, and for all he knew. He was taken to the stadium and faced a howling crowd clamoring for his death: "That teacher of Asia! That father-figure of the Christians! That destroyer of our gods!" Before too long Polycarp was condemned by an

---

[3] St Irenaeus of Lyons, *Against Heresies* 3, 3, 4 (AD 180).
[4] *The Demurrer Against the Heretics* 32 (c. AD 199).

intimidated Pro-consul after refusing to curse Christ: "How can I blaspheme my King who has saved me?" At first, the flames miraculously did not consume him; St Polycarp dying only after a dagger was plunged into him:

> "And then we who were privileged to witness it saw a wondrous sight ... The fire took on the shape of a hollow chamber, like a ship's sail when the wind fills it, and formed a wall round about the martyr's figure ... Finally, when they realized that his body could not be destroyed by fire, the ruffians ordered one of the dagger-men to go up and stab him with his weapon" (*Martyrdom* 15:1; 16).

St Polycarp wrote many letters, however, all that remains extant is his *Letter to the Philippians*, which is actually a composite of two letters written c. AD 110 and 135 respectively. The Philippians had expressed a desire to receive spiritual advice from St Polycarp so he responded with earnest warnings against the love of money and the Docetist heresy: "Everyone who does not confess that Jesus Christ has come in the flesh is an Antichrist; whoever does not confess the testimony of the cross, is of the devil ..." (*The Letter(s) to the Philippians* 7:1). In addition, there are instructions on the proper duties of presbyters and deacons as well as lay men and women.

St Polycarp was not an original writer but was steadfast in passing on the Apostolic truths he learned in his youth. He had a simple pious sense of the faith and reacted instinctively against any form of heresy. In his later years he was pained to see the widespread growth of false doctrine and cried out, "O good God, what sort of era have you preserved me for, that I have to suffer such things as this!"[5]

After the death of St Polycarp, his faithful congregation in Smyrna were asked to give a full outline of the event by members of the church of Philomelium. One of the actual witnesses, a certain Marcion, accordingly compiled what is now acknowledged as the earliest authentic record of a Christian martyrdom. The *Martyrdom of Polycarp* is written in a true story-teller's style and graphically describes the bishop's arrest and execution, making the reader feel part of the unfolding drama. This work became the

---

[5] Eusebius, *The History of the Church* 5, 20.

model for the many pious martyrologies of the subsequent second and third centuries.

The following extract from the *Martyrdom* tells us how well the memory and love for St Polycarp lived on in the Church in Asia Minor:

> "Christ we worship as the Son of God, but the martyrs we love as disciples and imitators of the Lord; and rightly so, because of their unsurpassable devotion to their own King and Teacher. With them may we also become companions and fellow disciples. When the centurion saw the contentiousness caused by the Jews, he confiscated the body, and, according to their custom, burned it. Then, at least, we took up his bones, more precious than costly gems and finer than gold, and put them in a suitable place. The Lord will permit us, when we are able, to assemble there in joy and gladness, and to celebrate the birthday of his martyrdom, both in memory of those who have already engaged in the contest, and for the practice and training of those who have yet to fight" (17:3).

Themes for study:
- St Ignatius' hatred of heresy and schism, his care for the unity of the Church, and in his great yearning for martyrdom.
- The significance of the Ignatian epistles.
- St Polycarp's long life linking the teachers and theologians of the mid-second century to the Apostolic founders of the Church.
- *The Martyrdom of Polycarp* as a model for future martyrologies.

Further reading:
- Warren H. Carroll, *The Founding of Christendom* (A History of Christendom), Vol. 1, Christendom Press, 1985, pp. 455-461.
- Fr John Laux, *Church History*, TAN Books and Publishers, 1930, pp. 48-50.
- Tixeront — Raemers, *A Handbook of Patrology*, B. Herder Book Co., 1946, pp. 13-17.
- Rev. William A. Jurgens, *The Faith of the Early Fathers*, The Liturgical Press, Collegeville, Minnesota, Vol. 1, pp. 17 & 28.

Hermas and St Justin Martyr

It is stated in the anonymous *Muratorian Fragment* (inter AD 155-200) that Hermas was the author of *The Shepherd* and the brother of Pope St Pius I who held the See of Peter from c. AD 140-155: "And very recently in our own times, in the city of Rome, Hermas wrote the Pastor, when his brother Pius, the bishop, sat upon the chair of the city of Rome." According to his autobiography, Hermas claimed to be a contemporary of St Clement of Rome, though the veracity of this reference is questionable.

Hermas was originally a Greek slave who later became a freedman after being sold to a Christian lady named Rhode. He then applied himself to business, amassing great wealth from his farm that lay between Rome and Cumae. Consequently, he neglected his spiritual life and, more particularly, failed to morally guide his wife and children. When persecution came, however, he and his wife confessed the faith only to be betrayed by their apostate children. Hermas' betrayal resulted in the loss of his fortune but led to his conversion to fervor. It was while endeavoring to do penance for the past that he composed *The Shepherd*.

The Shepherd was most probably written in Rome during the reign of St Pius I. Its purpose was to call clergy and laity responsible for grave disorders in the Roman Church to penance. The necessity of penance, its efficacy and its conditions form the groundwork of the work. Hermas presents his ideas as a seer passing on visions and revelations that have been given to him by "the Matron." This was done so that his readers would more readily accept his ideas. There are two distinct personages who appear to Hermas. The first is the Church in the form of an aged woman ("the Matron") who grows younger and more graceful with each vision; the second is the Angel of Penance to whose care Hermas has been entrusted.

The Shepherd is divided into three parts, namely, five *Visions*, twelve *Commandments*, and ten *Parables*. Together, they insist upon virtues and good works, faith, fear of the Lord, chastity, simplicity, patience, temperance, truthfulness, and the discernment of true and false prophets. Hermas was not a man of great culture or depth of learning, but possessed the qualities of an excellent moralist with a deep sense of divine mercy. St Irenaeus, Tertullian (while a Catholic), Clement of Alexandria and Origen considered *The Shepherd* to be an inspired work of a true prophet, though not a canonical work. Eusebius and St Athanasius approved it for use by Catechumens; in contrast, St Jerome ridiculed parts of it. It was often appended to New Testament manuscripts and achieved a great deal of good in the early centuries, however, it dwindled in popularity both in the East and West from the fourth century onwards. The decree of Pope Gelasius (AD 496) listed it among the apocryphal books.

St Justin Martyr was the first of the outstanding apologists of the Church and the greatest of the second century. He was born of Roman pagan parents in Flavia Neapolis (ancient Sichem in Palestine) some time after AD 100. St Justin in his youth was attracted to and studied all the major systems of philosophy, and at one stage or another was a Stoic, Peripatetic, Pythagorean and Platonist. However, none of these philosophies gave peace to his soul. Encountering an aged Christian in a lonely place (perhaps in Ephesus), St Justin was advised to study Christianity and pray for light to know Christ and true wisdom. He took the advice and embraced Christianity around AD 130: "This Christian philosophy alone was sure and profitable."

We know of St Justin's life mostly through his own writings. He always wore the mantle of a philosopher, and in his prolific writing and itinerant preaching defended the teaching of Christ as the highest and most perfect philosophy against both Jews and Pagans. He was the first to study the relation between faith and reason and introduced Greek philosophical terminology into his expositions.

He was admired for his earnest convictions, noble character and perfect loyalty in his dealings. He was an apostle and saint in the true sense of the words. After spending time teaching in Ephesus, St Justin moved to Rome and there set up a successful Christian school, having Tatian the Syrian as one of his students.

Of all his writings only three have survived substantially intact, namely his two *Apologies* and the *Dialogue with Trypho the Jew*. St Justin wrote his apologies to the Emperor Antoninus Pius, his adopted sons and to the Roman Senate explaining and defending Christian faith and practice. In his works we find the first open written account of the

Christian mysteries, particularly baptism and the Eucharist, hitherto kept under wraps by the "discipline of the secret":

> "And this food is called among us the Eucharist, of which no one is allowed to partake but the man who has been washed in the washing bath that is for the remission of sins, and unto regeneration, and who is so living as Christ has enjoined. For not as common bread nor common drink do we receive these; but since Jesus Christ our Savior was made incarnate by the word of God and had both flesh and blood for our salvation, so too, as we have been taught, the food which has been made into the Eucharist by the Eucharistic prayer set down by Him, and by the change of which our blood and flesh is nourished is both the flesh and the blood of that incarnated Jesus ... The Apostles, in the Memoirs which they produced, which are called Gospels, have thus passed on that which was enjoined upon them: that Jesus took bread and, having given thanks, said, 'Do this in remembrance of Me; this is My Body.' And in like manner, taking the cup, and having given thanks, He said, 'This is My Blood.' And He imparted this to them only."[1]

St Justin was also the first to write of the Virgin Mary as the "New Eve":

> "He became Man by the Virgin so that the course which was taken by disobedience in the beginning through the agency of the serpent, might be also the very course by which it would be put down. For Eve, a virgin and undefiled, conceived the word of the serpent, and bore disobedience and death. But the Virgin Mary received faith and joy when the angel Gabriel announced to her the glad tidings that the Spirit of the Lord would come upon her and the power of the Most High would overshadow her, for which reason the Holy One being born of her is the Son of God. And she replied: 'Be it done unto me according to thy word.'"[2]

St Justin wrote convincingly to dispel the widely spread calumnies that Christians were atheists, cannibals and sexually immoral (*concubitus oedipodei, epulae thyesteae*). The Christians were not only moral, but also

---

[1] *First Apology* 66 (c. AD 155).
[2] *Dialogue with Trypho the Jew* 100 (c. AD 160).

loyal to all legitimate authority and therefore deserving of tolerance: "And if these things seem to you to be reasonable and true, honor them; but if they seem nonsensical, despise them as nonsense, and do not decree death against those who have done no wrong, as you would enemies" (*First Apology* 68). Christians were persecuted only out of ignorance and misapprehension, stirred on by the Demons. Unfortunately St Justin's hope of getting the Emperor to repeal the anti-Christian laws had no effect.

The *Dialogue with Trypho the Jew* is the oldest known apologetical work against Judaism. Trypho was probably a historical person, a learned Rabbi of some note who openly debated with St Justin at Ephesus between AD 132-135. The *Dialogue* was written around AD 160 as a record of the disputation that lasted two days.

There exist also four fragments of another treatise entitled *On the Resurrection*. Various patristic writers ascribe this work to St Justin, including St John Damascene. Whether or not it is an authentic work of St Justin it is undoubtedly ancient, being alluded to by Methodius of Olympus at the end of the third century. St Justin is reputed to have authored a vast number of other works, including a *Discourse Against the Greeks*, all of which have been lost.

According to the authentic *Martyrdom of Sts Justin and Sociorum*, St Justin and six companions were denounced to the authorities as Christians in the fourth year of the reign of Marcus Aurelius (AD 165), perhaps by his adversary, the cynic Crescens. After being tried and condemned by the Prefect Junius Rusticus, all seven were scourged and beheaded by sword. St Justin's last recorded words were, "It is our heart's desire to be martyred for Our Lord Jesus Christ and then to be happy forever." Eusebius referred to St Justin as "an ornament of our Faith soon after the Apostles' time" (*The History of the Church* 2:13).

Themes for study:
- The value of *The Shepherd of Hermas* in the early Church.
- St Justin's study of the relationship between faith and reason and introduction of Greek philosophical terminology into his expositions.
- St Justin's spirited defense of Christianity before the Emperor, breaking with the tradition of the "discipline of the secret".

- St Justin's sincere life as a Christian and his betrayal and martyrdom.

Further reading:
- Fr John Laux, *Church History*, TAN Books and Publishers, 1930, pp. 57-59.
- Tixeront – Raemers, *A Handbook of Patrology*, B. Herder Book Co., 1946, pp. 23-27; 35-40.
- Rev. William A. Jurgens, *The Faith of the Early Fathers*, The Liturgical Press, Collegeville, Minnesota, Vol. 1, pp. 32-33; 50.
- Patrick J. Hamell, *Handbook of Patrology*, Alba House, 1968, pp. 32-34; 38-40.

St Irenaeus of Lyons and the Gnostic Heresy

St Irenaeus (Irenaeus="Peacemaker") was born in Asia Minor around AD 140. He was a native of Smyrna where in his adolescent years he was acquainted with St Polycarp. During this time, he became an assiduous disciple of the aged bishop and would later appeal to his authority.

St Irenaeus was brought to Rome in the summer of AD 154 by St Polycarp, who came to discuss to date for celebrating Easter with Pope Anicetus. St Irenaeus remained in Rome after his mentor returned to Asia Minor, studying and later teaching. Sometime later, St Irenaeus moved westwards to Lyons. The reasons for this move lay probably in the fact that the Christian community in Lyons was mostly made up of emigrants from Asia Minor who knew St Polycarp.

In the summer of AD 177, a fierce persecution broke out against the Christians of Lyons, the likes of which had been unseen since the days of Nero. So fierce was the persecution that the bodies of the victims were all burnt to ashes and thrown into the Rhone River "that they might not even have hope of resurrection." Not even the ninety-year old Bishop St Pothinus was spared, being beaten to death. During this savagery, St Irenaeus, now a presbyter, was sent to Rome with a letter for Pope Eleutherius concerning the influence of Montanism, and others for the brethren back in Phrygia, Asia Minor. When St Irenaeus later returned to Lyons it was as its second bishop, and at only the tender age of thirty-seven years.

St Irenaeus stands out in history for a number of important reasons: firstly, he was involved (c. AD 190) in trying to forestall Pope Victor I from excommunicating Polycrates of Ephesus and the entire East over the date for the celebration of Easter; secondly, he combated Gnosticism through his compiling of *Against Heresies*, a work which ranks him as certainly the most important theologian of the second century (Jurgens vol. 1, p. 84). Tertullian called Irenaeus "a curious explorer of all doctrines", while others have called him the "Father of Catholic

Theology"; thirdly, he labored zealously for the conversion of the countryside around Lyons.

St Irenaeus wrote *Against Heresies* at the request of a friend, perhaps a bishop, who desired an exposition of heresies he was unfamiliar with. The full name for *Against Heresies* is *The Detection and Overthrow of the Gnosis Falsely So-called.* This enormous five-volume work was originally written entirely in Greek between the years AD 180 and 199. St Irenaeus' exposition of the Gnostic systems is sincere and well-informed. Up until certain discoveries of Gnostic writings in the mid-1940's the *Against Heresies* was the primary source for knowledge of Gnostic beliefs. Hamell in his work gives a succinct outline of these beliefs:

> "God was distinguished from the Demiurge, Maker of the World, and there was a hierarchy of Aeons or inferior gods. (1) There is one God, separate from matter (eternal), the first syzygy, (a couple, male and female), being produced by God himself directly, and it produced a second — the complete series of aeons being the Pleroma. As they recede from God the aeons become less perfect, one finally goes astray, is cast out into a lower world and peoples it with fresh aeons, and the declension in good continues. This rejected aeon finally creates the material world — it is the Demiurge, the God of the Jews and of evil. (3) Man is not entirely corrupt. A divine seed or spark detached from the higher world by the higher aeons was introduced into matter where the Demiurge kept it prisoner and persecuted it. (4) Redemption aims at delivering the divine spark in matter."[1]

The first volume of *Against Heresies* deals with the detection of the errors of the various Gnostic sects, the second and fifth are devoted to refuting these errors. In the fifth book are also found St Irenaeus' Chiliastic theories (millennialism). The third book outlines the rule of faith for Christians, which is the teaching of the Apostles preserved and passed on in its integrity by the Church. The fourth book contains arguments from both the Old and New Testaments, with a confirmation of the divine origin of the Old Testament against the Marcionites. In refuting his opponents, St Irenaeus is never overawed by their pretentious

---

[1] Patrick J. Hamell, *Handbook of Patrology*, Alba House, 1968, p. 47.

abstractions, and at times even mocks their follies with a malicious pleasure.

St Irenaeus endeavored to expose the Gnostic claim of special knowledge revealed only to "the perfect" as foreign to Apostolic tradition. The true faith is that given to the Apostles and passed on to the whole Church through the succession of bishops. The succession of the Bishops of Rome is outlined because of her primacy (*potior principalitas*) due to being founded by Sts Peter and Paul. Rome's doctrine passed on from the time of St Peter is conclusive proof of Christian faith. The principles St Irenaeus established concerning the doctrinal authority of the Church, and of Rome in particular, amount also to a refutation in advance of future heresies:

> "When, therefore, we have such proofs, it is not necessary to seek among others the truth which is easily obtained from the Church. For the Apostles, like a rich man in a bank, deposited with her most copiously everything which pertains to the truth; and everyone whosoever wishes draws from her the drink of life. For she is the entrance to life, while all the rest are thieves and robbers. That is why it is surely necessary to avoid them, while cherishing with the utmost diligence the things pertaining to the Church, and to lay hold of the tradition of truth ... In the Church, God has placed apostles, prophets and doctors, and all the other means through which the Spirit works; in all of which none have any part who do not conform to the Church. On the contrary, they defraud themselves of life by their wicked opinion and most wretched behavior. For where the Church is, there is the Spirit of God; and where the Spirit of God, there the Church and every grace (3:3:1)."

The office of Peter, Papal succession, and the preservation of Apostolic tradition:

> "The successions of the bishops of the greatest and most ancient Church known to all, founded and organized at Rome by the two most glorious Apostles, Peter and Paul, that Church which has the tradition and the faith which comes down to us after having been announced to men by the Apostles. For with this the whole world; and it is in her that the faithful everywhere have

maintained the Apostolic tradition ... The blessed Apostles (Peter and Paul), having founded and built up the Church (of Rome), they handed over the office of the episcopate to Linus. Paul makes mention of this Linus in the Epistle to Timothy. To him succeeded Anacletus; and after him, in the third place from the Apostles, Clement was chosen for the episcopate ... In this order, and by the teaching of the Apostles handed down in the Church, the preaching of the truth has come down to us (3:3:2-3)."

"If there should be a dispute over some kind of question, ought we not have recourse to the most ancient Churches in which the Apostles were familiar, and draw from them what is clear and certain in regard to that question? What if the Apostles had not in fact left writings to us? Would it not be necessary to follow the order of tradition, which was handed down to those to whom they entrusted the Churches? (3:4:1)."

The Blessed Virgin Mary as the New Eve:

"(Eve) having become disobedient, was made the cause of death for herself and for the whole human race; so also Mary, betrothed to a man but nevertheless still a virgin, being obedient, was made the cause of salvation for herself and for the whole human race ... Thus, the knot of Eve's disobedience was loosed by the obedience of Mary. What the virgin Eve had bound in unbelief, the Virgin Mary loosed through faith (3:22:4)."

The Eucharist as the actual Body and Blood of Christ:

"He took that created thing, bread, and gave thanks and said, 'This is My Body.' And the cup likewise, which is part of that creation to which we belong, He confessed to be His Blood, and taught the new oblation of the new covenant, which the Church, receiving from the Apostles, offers to God throughout the world ... concerning which Malachy, among the twelve prophets thus spoke beforehand: 'From the rising of the sun to the going down, My name is glorified among the gentiles, and in every place incense is offered to My name and a pure sacrifice' ... indicating in the plainest manner that in every place sacrifice shall be offered to Him, and at that a pure one (4:17:5)."

"If the body be not saved, then, in fact, neither did the Lord redeem us with His Blood; and neither is the cup of the Eucharist the partaking of His Blood nor is the Bread which we break the partaking of His Body ... He has declared the cup, a part of creation, to be His own Blood, from which He causes our blood to flow; and the bread, a part of creation, He has established as His own Body, from which gives increase to our bodies (5:2:2)."

Other works of St Irenaeus include the recently discovered treatise *Demonstration of the Apostolic Teaching*, which contains an exposition and proof of the truth of principal Christian dogmas for the ordinary faithful; a letter *On the Monarchy of God* which contains the teachings of St Polycarp against God as the author of evil; and other letters, namely, *On the Ogdoad*, *On Schism*, *On Science*, and fragments contained in Eusebius (*The History of the Church* 5:16; 19:1) of letters to Pope Victor on the Easter question.

After the incident between Pope Victor and Polycrates, St Irenaeus drops out of the limelight. According to St Jerome (*Commentary on Isaiah*) and St Gregory of Tours (*History of the Franks*), he died a martyr's death around AD 202 in the general massacres of Christians under Septimus Severus, though Eusebius, who possessed a good knowledge of St Irenaeus' life, makes no mention of this.

Themes for study:
- St Irenaeus as the student of, and heir to, St Polycarp's teaching.
- St Irenaeus as Bishop of Lyons.
- St Irenaeus' writing of *Against Heresies* and his struggle against Gnosticism.
- Apostolic tradition as passed on by the Bishops of Rome as the rule of faith.

Further reading:
- Fr John Laux, *Church History*, TAN Books and Publishers, 1930, pp. 60-62.
- Tixeront – Raemers, A *Handbook of Patrology*, B. Herder Book Co., 1946, pp. 77-80.

- Rev. William A. Jurgens, *The Faith of the Early Fathers*, The Liturgical Press, Collegeville, Minnesota, Vol. 1, p. 84.
- Patrick J. Hamell, *Handbook of Patrology*, Alba House, 1968, pp. 47; 51-55.

The Catechetical School of Alexandria

The Catechetical School of Alexandria was founded about AD 180 by Pantaenus, of whom little is known. What is known of him is given by Eusebius in his *History of the Church* (5:10-11): he was a Hebrew of Palestine who traveled to Egypt and there studied Stoic philosophy. Afterwards, he impressed his knowledge of the Greek philosophers into the service of Christianity. During his twenty years at the helm of his school he also traveled to the East, reaching southern Arabia or even India. There, he found Christians possessing the Gospel of St Matthew in Hebrew, given them by the Apostle Bartholomew. Pantaenus died around AD 200 and was succeeded by his earnest disciple, Clement of Alexandria. Clement would later refer to his mentor as "a Hebrew of Palestine, greater than all the others in ability, whom having hunted out in his concealment in Egypt, I found rest."

Clement of Alexandria was born of pagan parents in Athens around AD 150. The circumstances concerning his conversion are unknown, but it is supposed that he was attracted to Christianity by the nobility and purity of its teachings. After his conversion, he traveled throughout southern Italy, Rome and then the Middle East seeking teachers to advance his Christian knowledge. It was in Alexandria that he met up with the celebrated Pantaenus and became a pupil in his catechetical school (c. AD 180). Eventually, Clement was ordained a presbyter and rose to succeed Pantaenus around AD 200.

After only a brief number of years (c. AD 203), Clement was forced to flee Egypt in the face of the persecution of Septimus Severus, making his way to Cappadocia. There, he met up with a former disciple, Bishop Alexander, and together they rendered faithful service to the people of the region. In AD 216, Bishop Alexander writes to Origen and speaks of Clement as having gone to his rest.

Clement possessed a broad and noble mind coupled with a sympathetic and noble character. He was very widely read and remembered much of what he encountered. No other ancient author knew or quoted as many pagan and Christian writers as he. As a writer, Clement's chief aim was to determine the relationship between faith and reason and to show what philosophy had achieved as a preparation for the coming of Christian Revelation. Philosophy is the tool by which the data given through Divine Revelation is to be transformed into a scientific theology.

Clement produced three great works:

(1) The *Exhortation to the Greeks* (or *Protreptikos*). This is an apologetical work aimed at showing the influence of the Logos, or Divine Word, throughout history in the education of humanity. It is in twelve chapters and attacks the worthlessness and falsity of pagan beliefs and the inadequacy of philosophy without God and the true religion found in the teachings of the Prophets and Jesus Christ;
(2) *The Instructor of Children* (or *Paidagogos*) is a three-part sequel to the *Exhortation* and opens with an attack on the false knowledge of the Gnostics. True knowledge, rather, is a development of faith that begins with the illuminative effects of baptism. Clement then proceeds to present the Logos as an instructor of converts, particularly in regard to the conduct of Christians in a pagan world;
(3) The *Miscellanies* (or *Stromateis*) is a collection of eight books in which Clement treats a whole variety of different topics. These include the legitimacy of studying philosophy and the sciences, the relations between faith and Christian gnosis, marriage, martyrdom, and the religious life of a Christian, etc.

Other significant works of Clement include the *Hypotyposes*, an eight-volume commentary on the Old and New Testaments and the *Quis Dives Salvetur?*, a homily on St Mark 10:17-31, filled with unction and pious reflections. Surviving fragments of other writings are mentioned by Eusebius.

Clement was succeeded at the helm of the Catechetical School by the renowned Origen. Origen was born around AD 185 of Christian parents in Alexandria. His father, St Leonidas, was martyred in AD 202 during the reign of Septimus Severus. It was in his teenage years that Origen became a disciple of Pantaenus and Clement and showed very early on that he possessed a mind of insatiable curiosity and diligence.

The Catechetical School of Alexandria

Though only eighteen years of age and a layman, Origen was given control of the Catechetical School by Bishop Demetrius after the exile of Clement. Between AD 204 and 230, Origen raised it to its greatest prominence. While teaching, though, he was still studying and acquired knowledge of Neo-Platonist philosophy and Hebrew. He grasped all the scriptural, theological and philosophical reasoning of his time.

Origen was the most prodigious writer of all time. He was above all a Scripture scholar and formulated almost his entire theology in his written commentaries on the sacred texts. A wealthy pupil of his, Ambrosius, placed at Origen's disposal an abundance of secretaries and copyists. St Jerome and Eusebius knew of some two thousand works produced by Origen. St Epiphanius gives the figure as six thousand. Such prodigiousness earned Origen the title of greatest scholar of Christian antiquity.

The major works of Origen can be briefly listed as follows:

(1) *The Hexalpa*: This work contained six different Hebrew and Greek versions of the Old Testament in six parallel columns to compare them so to detect at a glance the true meaning of a passage;
(2) *The Scholia*: Briefs notes on the more difficult passages of Scripture;
(3) *The Homilies*: Familiar talks with the faithful on the Scriptures;
(4) *The Commentaries*: Written works to explain the texts of the Scriptures in a scientific way to his readers;
(5) *Against Celsus*: An apologetical work against the Platonist Celsus who had launched a learned and caustic attack against Christianity;
(6) *Fundamental Doctrines*: An early Summa Theologica in four volumes aimed at bringing together the fundamental teachings of Christianity and treating them in a systematic way.

Due to the persecution of Emperor Caracalla in AD 215, Origen left Alexandria and made his way to Caesarea in Palestine. There, Bishops Theoctistus and Alexander allowed him to preach to the congregation on Scripture, to the ire of Bishop Demetrius of Alexandria who demanded Origen's return to Egypt.

Fifteen years later, Origen again passed through Caesarea, and in order to pre-empt any objections to his preaching, Bishops Theoctistus and Alexander ordained him to the priesthood. This was in violation of the canons and thoroughly enraged Bishop Demetrius, who then convoked two synods in Alexandria in AD 230 and 231 that deposed, degraded and excommunicated Origen. Bishop Demetrius then sent special letters to all the other major churches notifying them of the measures taken.

Banished from Alexandria, Origen then moved to Caesarea where he founded and ran a school in the style of that of Alexandria for over twenty years. One of his famous pupils there was St Gregory Thaumaturgus. Origen survived the persecution of Emperor Thrax (AD 235-237) but during the Decian persecution he was arrested, imprisoned and tortured, dying as a result of his sufferings in Tyre in 253 or 254 at the age of sixty-nine.

During his lifetime, Origen was never suspected of heresy. He was always acknowledged as a great scholar and theologian who always endeavored to be faithful to Catholic teaching. The controversies that arose over his writings occurred on three separate occasions at the beginning of the fourth, fifth and sixth centuries. Origen was subsequently declared to have taught error and certain propositions of his declared formally heretical. This accounts for the large-scale destruction and loss of many of his writings, as well as many other expurgations, interpolations and retranslations. We now possess a little more than one-hundredth of what he produced, and this of poor quality and preservation.

Another great and the final head of the Catechetical School was Didymus the Blind. Didymus was born in Alexandria around AD 313. Although becoming blind at the age of four, he never prayed for the return of his sight but for illumination of the heart. Didymus developed an insatiable desire for knowledge and through an indomitable will became one of the most learned men of his time.

Appointed head of the Catechetical School by the great St Athanasius, Didymus had as his more famous students and hearers St Antony of the Desert, Palladius, Evaigrius Ponticus, St Jerome and Rufinus of Aquilaea. St Jerome often spoke of Didymus not as the blind but as "the Seer." Didymus remained head of the Catechetical School for over half a century.

Probably as a consequence of his blindness, Didymus was able to develop a prolific memory and gained a vast knowledge of philosophy and theology as well as other secular sciences. He was also noted for his exceptional kindness and angelic disposition. His fame spread far and wide. The orator Libanius wrote to an Egyptian official: "You cannot surely be ignorant of Didymus, unless you are ignorant of the great city wherein he has night and day been pouring out his learning for the good of others." The tone of his writings is always well balanced and calculated to win over his opponent rather than to defeat him. He always railed against the heresy but never the heretic. Thus, he had friends even among the Arians.

Didymus was never ordained, remaining instead a layman living a life of austerity in relative isolation outside Alexandria. He has, however, never been accorded the title of saint due to Origenist opinions concerning the pre-existence of souls and the ultimate salvation of all in his writings. This unfortunate circumstance is the reason why his name appears side by side with that of Origen in the condemnation of the Third Council of Constantinople in AD 680.

His condemnation also explains why much of what Didymus composed has also been lost. His voluminous exegetical works on most of the Old and New Testament books have virtually all disappeared. So, too, his dogmatic works. Besides a few fragments discovered here and there, only two works remain – his treatise on the Holy Spirit and his three books on the Trinity. The former was extensively used by St Ambrose in his own work on the Holy Spirit and survives in St Jerome's Latin translation; the latter is Didymus' principal work and has survived intact probably due to being free of Origenism.

After a life devoted to prayer, penance and work, Didymus died peacefully in AD 398 at the age of eighty-five. Soon after, the Catechetical School of Alexandria moved to Side where it failed to meet success and closed permanently.

Themes for study:
- The founding of the Catechetical School by Pantaenus.
- The elevation to prominence of the Catechetical School by Clement.
- The brilliance and prodigiousness of Origen.
- Didymus the Blind as the last head of the Catechetical School.

Further reading:
- *The Catholic Encyclopaedia* (1911, vol. XI, pp. 446-447).
- Philip Hughes, *A History of the Church*, Vol. 1, Sheed and Ward, 1948, pp. 118-128.
- Fr John Laux, *Church History*, TAN Books and Publishers, 1930, pp. 68-70.
- Tixeront – Raemers, *A Handbook of Patrology*, B. Herder Book Co., 1946, pp. 84-89, 158-160.

AD 201 to AD 300: THE PERSECUTIONS AND THE POPES

Heresy and Schism in the Pontificate of St Callistus I

Gnosticism was by no means the only heresy plaguing the Church during the second century. Heretics and their heresies began to abound everywhere: the Adoptionists[1], Modalists[2], and Ditheists[3]. Another serious heresy was Montanism.

Montanism had its remote origins in the wild Phrygian countryside in central Asia Minor some time during the AD 170's. This heresy received its name from its founder, Montanus, a former priest of the pagan goddess Cybele. Together with two women followers, Priscilla and Maximilla, Montanus taught a version of Christianity that combined enthusiasm with rigorous ritual purity. As a part of his repertoire, Montanus would utter alleged prophesy and claimed to 'speak in tongues.'

Montanist spirituality was heavily centered on the supposed coming end of the world. To meet this climactic event, Montanus encouraged his followers to practise the most extreme asceticism, including

---

[1] The Adoptionists taught that Christ was inferior to the Father, being only a creature and becoming the adopted Son of God only at his baptism.

[2] This heresy, otherwise known as Monarchianism or Patripassianism, advocated that there were not three distinct Persons in the one God, but that God was one Person who manifested Himself in three different 'modes.'

[3] Ditheism advocated that the Father and the Son were two separate Gods.

severe fasting. Montanist preachers called upon their listeners to renounce all marriage, especially second marriages, to abandon worldly possessions, and foreswear all civil obligations. On the other hand, flight from persecution was forbidden and martyrdom was actively encouraged. The 'faithful remnant' was called upon to live together in the obscure Phrygian town of Pepuza, the so-called 'New Jerusalem', where Montanus' followers adhered to his every word as the utterances of the Holy Spirit Himself. Though finding virtually no support among bishops, Montanus was able to find receptive ears from all over Asia Minor. The whole church of Thyatira, for example, became entirely Montanistic.

At first, the Montanists were considered to be no more than an aberration, posing no great danger to warrant a formal condemnation by the Pope at the time, Eleutherius. However, by the early AD 190's matters began to change. The political calamities that beset Rome between AD 193 and 197 gave strength to heretics and schismatics who proclaimed the imminent end of the world, especially the Montanists. Even the condemnation of the Montanists in AD 201 by Pope Zephyrinus did not slow down their growth, let alone bring greater peace to the internal life of the Church.

Nor was peace forthcoming externally either. One year later, in AD 202, Emperor Septimus Severus launched his own persecution of Christianity, expressly forbidding anyone to convert to it. He may have been incited into such a move by the annoying prevalence of apocalyptic preaching by the Montanists, which he could not distinguish from mainstream Christianity. Nevertheless, Montanism continued to prosper, and in AD 213 gained one of its greatest coups, the conversion of the theologian and apologist Tertullian of Africa.

Tertullian's full name was Quintus Septimius Florens Tertullianus. He was born of pagan parents in Carthage just after the first half of the second century AD. As a youth, Tertullian's life was not virtuous but it was laborious. He read intensely and studied whatever he could lay his hands upon. He became a lawyer of considerate repute, and after his conversion (c. AD 193) he employed his considerable talents for the service and defense of Christianity. We do not know the circumstances of his conversion but we do know that it was sincere and thorough.

Tertullian was a born fighter with an energetic mind and iron will. He fought continuously for what he believed to be right and good, waging incessant war against heresy and paganism. Tertullian's greatest works include the *Apology* and the *Demurrer Against the Heretics*. In the former he defends Christianity against the unjust legal measures taken against it and makes his famous declaration that *"The blood of the martyrs is the seed of the Church."* In the latter he makes a general refutation of all dogmatic innovations through an affirmation of tradition and the authority of the Church.

Unfortunately, Tertullian lacked moderation and tended to exaggeration, making him susceptible to extremism. His firmness often descended into stubbornness, a telltale sign of pride. From AD 207 onwards he gradually drifted towards Montanism. His formal break with the Church came with Rome's allowance to contract second marriages after the death of the first spouse. Tertullian then turned his apologetical pen against the Church, falling into an extreme anticlericalism and invective. In his work *De Pudicitia* Tertullian responded to Pope Callistus' decree allowing the reception of the sacrament of Penance for mortal sexual sins by declaring that it should be "posted on the doors of brothels." In the same work he sarcastically dismissed *The Shepherd of Hermas* as the "Shepherd of Adulterers" for speaking of further opportunities for repentance for all sins committed after baptism.

In AD 217, Pope Zephyrinus died and was succeeded by his loyal friend and adviser Callistus. Callistus was a former slave of a fellow Christian named Carpophorus, who worked in the household of the Emperor Commodus. In this capacity he mismanaged his master's funds in a banking fraud and fled in panic. Soon Callistus was arrested, and denounced as a Christian by Jews to whom he had lent money, was sentenced to the salt mines of Sardinia. After a number of years, Callistus was freed as part of a general amnesty for Christian prisoners obtained by the Emperor's mistress, Marcia. Callistus would gain friendship and favor with Pope Zephyrinus through his considerable talents and the Pope placed him in charge of the Church's catacomb cemeteries. It was probably the local Roman clergy who nominated Callistus to the position of Archdeacon in AD 216 and then elected him Pope a year later. As Pope, Callistus had to contend not only with the polemical attacks of Tertullian but those also of the first antipope, St Hippolytus.

Not much is known of St Hippolytus' early life besides the fact that there is evidence that he was of eastern origin, probably born in

Alexandria between AD 170 and 175. He claimed to be a disciple of St Irenaeus of Lyons. By AD 212, Hippolytus was establishing a reputation in Rome as a presbyter and scholar. He was undoubtedly a man of great talent with skills in exegesis, apology, dogma, morals, discipline, history and geography. Above all he was an exegete. As a preacher and homilist he exhibited true oratorical ability with a style that was clear and elegant. However, at times he became irascible, as was evident in his controversies against Pope Callistus.

During the reign of Pope Zephyrinus, St Hippolytus opposed his solution to the Modalist heresy, a solution devised with the help of his adviser Callistus (St Hippolytus' own Christology was questionable, being suspect of Ditheism). When Callistus was later elected Pope, St Hippolytus opposed him openly in his work the *Philosophumena* for his alleged leniency towards repentant adulterers and fornicators, advocating a much more rigorous attitude. Gathering together a small group of devotees, St Hippolytus formed his own church and had himself elected as Bishop of Rome in opposition to Callistus, thus becoming the first antipope and affecting a formal schism.

Though Tertullian and St Hippolytus subscribed to different teachings, they both shared the denial of ecclesial absolution (then known as the *Exomologesis*) to those who had committed mortal sins of the flesh after baptism. In this they were upholding various rigorous customs that developed during the second century. One custom would deny absolution for all serious sins committed after baptism; another deny absolution only for murder, idolatry, apostasy, adultery and fornication; another only for adultery and fornication; another allow absolution for all mortal sins but only once, or twice. Persons guilty of such post-baptismal sins were no longer part of the Church. Rather, they were reduced for the rest of their lives to the level of penitents, left to the mercy of God.

On the other hand, Pope Callistus never waivered from the Church's long-held practice of reconciling sinners and forgiving "seventy times seven." During his short reign of five years, he bore the caustic attacks patiently and is renowned not only for confirming the availability of confession and absolution for all post-baptismal mortal sins, but also for recognizing the validity of marriages before God contracted by Christian women of higher rank with Christian men of social inferiority, even though such marriages were unrecognized in Roman law. For this act he earned the greater scorn of the rebel intellectuals and puritanical extremists. Nevertheless, he laid the foundation for the noble teachings that the availability of the sacraments is always independent of social position and the authority of the State.

Ironically, it is through the bitter attacks of his foes that the true greatness of Pope Callistus shines forth. What he was condemned for is now his glory: his saneness, solidity, love and forgiveness. In the end (14 October, AD 222) he was rewarded with the martyr's crown, being set upon by a raging mob and thrown to his death from a height. His body was then dumped in a well before being retrieved by his followers and buried in the cemetery of Calepodius on the Aurelian Way.

St Hippolytus would return to the Church after eighteen years in schism, inspired by the humility and example of another great Bishop of Rome, St Pontian, with whom he worked side by side in the salt mines. St Hippolytus has the dual distinction of being the first and only canonized antipope. On the other hand, the rigorous and unforgiving Tertullian would die an obscure death, unrecorded and uncelebrated. Some authors are of the view that he so dominated Montanism that the sect later became known as the Tertullianists. Records indicate that this sect subsisted until the end of the fourth century when St Augustine converted them.

Themes for study:
- The rise of the Montanist heresy.
- Tertullian's apostasy to Montanism.
- St Hippolytus as the first antipope and schismatic.
- The pastoral balance of Pope Callistus and his patience in the face of hostility.

Further reading:
- Warren H. Carroll, *The Founding of Christendom* (A History of Christendom), Vol. 1, Christendom Press, 1985, pp. 464-470.
- Fernard Hayward, *A History of the Popes*, J.M. Dent & Sons Ltd., 1931, pp. 26-29.
- Philip Hughes, *A History of the Church*, Vol. 1, Sheed and Ward, 1948, pp. 100-108.
- Fr John Laux, *Church History*, TAN Books and Publishers, 1930, pp. 63-64.

The Persecutions of Maximinus Thrax and Decius

During the first decades of the third century AD, Christianity again began to appear within the ranks of the Imperial ruling family. Septimus Severus, though having launched a persecution against Christianity himself, had a Christian as foster-mother to his son and heir, Caracalla. Later, through Septimus' wife, Syrians were to rise to the Roman throne, one being Alexander Severus at the age of thirteen in AD 222. His mother, the Empress Julia Mammaea, had summoned Origen to preach to her on the Christian mysteries while still in Antioch. St Hippolytus also dedicated his treatise *On the Resurrection* to her. As her son, Alexander also picked up some of Julia's interest in Christianity. Though always a syncretist, Alexander admired the teachings of Christ, placed a statue of him next to those of Orpheus and past Emperors in his oratory, and even planned to build a temple in his honor.

Under such rulers, some modification to the Roman anti-Christian laws was inevitable. Alexander abrogated the ancient law of Nero and granted Christians for the first time the right to exist. Christians could now also own property and erect places of worship. However, many within the ranks of Roman power resented these changes, as well as Alexander's general weak and cowardly nature and the overbearing influence of his mother Julia. The coup came from the ranks of the army, led by Maximinus Thrax, a rough and illiterate soldier of huge stature who murdered Alexander and seized the Emperorship of Rome in AD 235.

Maximinus was no lover of Christianity and immediately began reversing the policies of his predecessor. He then decreed a persecution against it aimed specifically at the hierarchy of Bishops. This persecution was novel in two respects: the State itself would hunt down its targets without waiting for denunciation; and it would apply universally throughout the Empire. Two of the decrees' first victims were Pope St Pontian and his rival to the papal throne St Hippolytus. Both were sent to the salt mines of Sardinia. Believing that he would never return to govern the Church from Rome, St Pontian resigned from his office, the first Pope to do so. This action may have impressed and humbled St Hippolytus, for soon after he abandoned his schism, received absolution from St Pontian, and sent a message to his followers to reconcile with the new Pope.

That Pope was Anteros, who lived for only six weeks after his elevation. He was sentenced to death by Roman imperial officials for having collected the acts of the martyrs and adding them to the Church's records. He was buried in the Catacombs and was succeeded by the simple farmer Fabian. Fabian would see the end of Thrax's persecution and rule the Church effectively for the next fourteen years. During that time, Pope Fabian had the relics of Pope Pontian placed in the Catacomb of Callistus, divided Rome into seven diaconal regions, kept a vigilant watch against heresy and sent missionaries into central and northern Gaul.

It was during the pontificate of St Fabian that Rome celebrated her millennium in AD 248. The Emperor at the time was Philip the Arab, a sympathizer of Christianity, perhaps even a Christian himself. The Church was enjoying a general respite from official persecution, though sporadic outbreaks of violence were occurring here and there. Further, the nature of the attack was also changing. Paganism now felt the need to combat Christianity by the pen as well as by the sword. The philosopher Celsus launched a comprehensive attack on Christianity, only to be refuted by the great Origen even more comprehensively. The fact that the pagan intelligentsia felt a need to make such an attack was an acknowledgement that Christianity possessed a life and strength that no sword could quash. On the other hand, the Empire of pagan Rome was moving ever faster towards her death throes through political disintegration, depopulation and the proliferation of competing religious sects.

One man who could sense the on-rushing death was the Roman senator Decius. He was a motivated and strong man who saw himself as the savior of Rome. In him was embodied all the old Roman conservatism and austerity. Unable to bear seeing Rome rot from within, he aimed to restore her as one, strong unity under the traditional gods. Eastern cults were no longer to be patronized; Christianity was to disappear. Four months after becoming Emperor, in January AD 250, Decius decreed that every man, woman and child in the Empire publicly sacrifice to the pagan gods or die. Since Christians were now a sizable part of the population, instructions were given to Governors to make every effort to persuade them to abjure their faith rather than be martyred. Those who stubbornly refused to conform would forfeit their property and perish.

The Decian persecution came as a shock to a Church that had enjoyed peace for most of the previous fifty years. The good relations with Alexander Severus and Philip the Arab tended to make many faithful believe that the struggle with paganism was virtually won. Much of the austerity and vigilance proper to times of persecution had waned, to the displeasure of men such as Origen and St Cyprian of Carthage. Again, the first victim of persecution was the Bishop of Rome, Pope Fabian, who was unhesitatingly targeted by Decius. Immediately after Fabian's death Decius declared that he hoped to never hear of the election of another Bishop of Rome.

Nor could a successor be elected as the persecution raged in earnest. Within just two months after its promulgation, Decius' decree claimed the lives of the Bishops of Rome, Carthage, Alexandria, Antioch, Jerusalem and Toulouse. The bishop of Smyrna apostatized, together with thousands of others throughout the Empire, especially Rome and North Africa.[1] Many others, including priests and bishops, went into hiding or took flight beyond the boundaries of the Empire. On the other hand, many great names were enrolled into the Acts of the Martyrs, names that have lived on throughout the centuries: the priest Pionius, Bishop Dionysius of Alexandria, Origen, Celerinus, Bishop Nestor of Pamphylia, Isidore and Agatha.

Success for Decius seemed imminent; the situation for the Christians, perilous. But at this same time Gothic barbarians crossed the Danube River and penetrated into the Balkans. Decius was forced to leave Rome with his army to meet the challenge. In his absence, the persecution was relaxed. Decius was defeated in his first encounter with the Goths in Thrace. In his second encounter at Dobrudja near the mouth of the Danube he vanished in the midst of the marshes, never to be seen again.

Decius' successor, Gallus, delayed continuing the persecution of

---

[1] There were various classes of apostates: the *Thurificati* – those that offered incense to the gods; the *Sacrificati* – those that offered sacrifice to the gods; the *Libellatici* – those who evaded persecution by dishonestly obtaining documents certifying that they had offered incense or sacrifice.

Christians for more than a year. In the interim, the surviving Roman clergy re-gathered and elected the humble Cornelius as Pope, passing over the distinguished and sophisticated Novatian. Stung by this, Novatian accused Cornelius of leniency in the re-admission of apostates back into the Church and set himself up as antipope. He then proceeded to take control of the entire Church by appointing new bishops throughout the Empire.

In response, Pope Cornelius summoned a synod of bishops, which met under his direction in Rome in the Autumn of AD 251. Sixty bishops debated and then proceeded to excommunicate Novatian and all his followers. They then laid down specific penitential requirements for readmitting the various categories of apostates back into the Church.

It was not long before the storm of persecution blew again. Gallus, moved by popular demand for a scapegoat because of plague affecting Rome, exiled Pope Cornelius into the Italian countryside, where he died in June AD 253. By then Gallus was also dead, overthrown by another army revolt now typical of the declining Empire. He was succeeded by Valerian.

Themes for study:
- The periods of Imperial favor towards Christianity under Alexander Severus and Philip the Arab.
- The nature and extent of the Thracian persecution.
- The suddenness and ferocity of the Decian persecution.
- The extent of apostasy during the Decian persecution.

Further reading:
- Warren H. Carroll, *The Founding of Christendom* (A History of Christendom), Vol. 1, Christendom Press, 1985, pp. 474-493.
- Fernard Hayward, *A History of the Popes*, J.M. Dent & Sons Ltd., 1931, pp. 29-33.
- Philip Hughes, *A History of the Church*, Vol. 1, Sheed and Ward, 1948, pp. 163-167.
- Fr John Laux, *Church History*, TAN Books and Publishers, 1930, pp. 66-68.

Pope St Stephen I and St Cyprian of Carthage

Pope Cornelius was succeeded by Lucius I in AD 253, who was in turn succeeded by St Stephen I just one year later. St Stephen was a Roman by birth, rose to the position of Archdeacon, and was appointed Pope by St Lucius I just before his martyrdom. St Stephen's pontificate would also be a short one, lasting just three years. It fell within the brief lull between the Decian and Valerian persecutions. Nevertheless, it was not without its dramas, the most notable being the growth of the schismatic Novatianists and St Stephen's clash with St Cyprian of Carthage over the re-baptism of heretics.

The Decian persecution had caused an unprecedented number of apostates, many of whom sought re-admission back into the Church after the storm. Pope Cornelius had already laid down a balanced policy for re-admission of the lapsed, one that was based on a procedure first implemented by St Cyprian in Africa. The main opposition came from the excommunicated antipope Novatian and his rigorist followers. They denied the power of the Church to absolve under any circumstance the lapsed through the *Exomologesis*. Apostates might repent and be admitted to a lifelong penance, but their forgiveness was to be left in the hands of God. The subsequent followers of Novatian would later extend refusal of the *Exomologesis* to all mortal sins, being influenced by the works of Tertullian. They also condemned second marriages and rebaptized Catholics who joined them.

The Novatianists had their own hierarchy, sacraments, churches and cemeteries. They eventually spread to every province, and in some places they were numerous. They called themselves the *Katapoi* (or Puritans). Lasting for centuries, this sect would be opposed by Sts Cyprian, Pacian of Barcelona, Ambrose and Augustine in the West, and Sts Epiphanius, Athanasius, Basil, Gregory Nazianzus and Chrysostom in the East. Pope Honorius in AD 412 included them in a law against heretics. Not long after, Pope St Celestine expelled them from Rome, as did St Cyril from Alexandria and Nestorius from Constantinople. Eulogius of

Alexandria during the late sixth century composed six books against them.

St Cyprian of Carthage was of that class of men who are born to rule. Coming from a socially distinguished family, he possessed a scholarly distinction and a courtesy to match. Decision-making, responsibility, and courage were all St Cyprian's by nature, so too the spirit of a practical controversialist. All these fine qualities shone through during the troubled years of Decius' persecution and the development of the Novatian schism. The treatise *On the Unity of the Church* was St Cyprian's great attempt to restore peace in the face of the growing schism: "Outside the Church there is no salvation. He cannot have God as his Father, who has not the Church for his Mother."

Two problems, however, were inherent in St Cyprian that remotely contributed to his dispute with Pope St Stephen. The first was that St Cyprian was a relatively recent convert and a newly consecrated bishop of only five years standing (since AD 248). He still had much to learn in the areas of philosophy and theology. His main readings were the writings of Tertullian, who he called *"Da Magistrum."* The second was the exaggerated sense of his own relative importance to the Bishop of Rome, which he may have gained while the Roman See was vacant during the height of persecution and the beginning of the Novatian schism. In some of St Cyprian's writings around this period are found passages stating that all bishops are equals and that it is the right of the local people to depose bishops who were sinners; in others he recognizes Rome as the *'Ecclesia Principalis'* and advocates, as well as urges, the Bishop of Rome to directly intervene to appoint or depose bishops in other cities (as was the case with the Novatianist bishop of Arles). There develops confusion also with respect to his teaching on baptism.

During the religious revival after the Decian persecution, a layman of some note addressed to St Cyprian the question of whether persons already baptized by heretics should be re-baptized when received into the Church. St Cyprian replied in writing, stating that baptism administered by heretics cannot be of value for the Holy Spirit does not operate outside the one true Church. Controversy soon developed and an opposition party to St Cyprian rose up quoting another practice no older than thirty years. In the Lent of AD 256, a meeting of all the bishops of Africa and Numidia re-affirmed St Cyprian's position, and St Cyprian proceeded to inform Rome of the council's decision.

Rome, together with Alexandria, had always taught that the baptism of heretics was valid. When St Cyprian's envoys arrived in Rome they found themselves treated as heretics. They were refused hospitality, communion and even a hearing. St Cyprian was regarded as a false prophet of a false Christ. Pope St Stephen, specifically noting his authority as successor to Peter, ordered St Cyprian and the African episcopate to stop re-baptizing persons originally baptized by heretics, on the grounds that baptism invoked in the name of the Trinity receives its efficacy to remit original sin from Christ and is not dependent on the worthiness or otherwise of the minister of the sacrament. Heretics already baptized were simply to be received, subject to the imposition of a penance. Sure of his position, Pope St Stephen published his decision throughout the whole Church.

St Cyprian refused to comply, arguing that the administration of baptism was a detail of the local church's life and that the question of the validity of baptism was one on which Catholic bishops can differ. St Cyprian attacked Pope St Stephen for his alleged "haughtiness, self-contradictions", and argued that "each bishop has the right to think for himself and as he is not accountable to any other, so is no bishop accountable to him" — statements in clear contradiction to his earlier ones affirming the primacy of St Peter's successor and the unity of the Church. The rest of the African bishops supported St Cyprian. St Cyprian also found support in Firmilian, Bishop of Caesarea in Cappadocia, who in the most scathing language accused the Pope of disturbing the peace of the Church and propagating heresy.

Before Rome could take any further action, Pope St Stephen died. The *Liber Pontificalis* states that his death was due to martyrdom, but the evidence for this is unreliable. His successor, Sixtus II, was of a milder disposition and a friend of St Cyprian. He took the decision not to immediately press the matter further due to the revival of persecution under the Emperor Valerian. St Dionysius, bishop of Alexandria, also made conciliatory moves.

Eleven months after Pope St Stephen's death, St Cyprian would also pass from this world, laying down his life for his faith (14 September AD 258). His *Acta* are among the most moving of that genre of literature, and record the serene beauty of his death: "Brought before the Proconsul and asked who he was, Cyprian replied: 'I am a Christian and a Bishop.'

When the sentence of death was pronounced, he said, 'Thanks be to God.'" Despite his disagreement and actual disobedience, St Cyprian was never excommunicated, and ironically, his name was entered among the list of martyrs and read out during the Mass together with the names of those Popes he sometimes opposed. As St Augustine would later say, "he merited to attain the crown of martyrdom, so that any cloud which had obscured the brightness of his mind was driven away by the brilliant sunshine of his glorious blood."

Themes for study:
- The growth of the Novatianist schism.
- St Cyprian's contradictory writings concerning the primacy of Rome and Church unity.
- St Cyprian's disobedience towards Pope St Stephen regarding the validity of baptism administered by heretics.
- St Cyprian's martyrdom and restoration to favor.

Further reading:
- Warren H. Carroll, *The Founding of Christendom* (A History of Christendom), Vol. 1, Christendom Press, 1985, pp. 494-495.
- Fernard Hayward, *A History of the Popes*, J.M. Dent & Sons Ltd., 1931, pp. 34-35.
- Philip Hughes, *A History of the Church*, Vol. 1, Sheed and Ward, 1948, pp. 112-118.
- Fr John Laux, *Church History*, TAN Books and Publishers, 1930, pp. 71-72.

The Persecutions of Valerian and Aurelian

Upon first coming to the imperial throne in AD 253 Valerian was friendly to the Christians, allowing Pope Lucius I to return to Rome and ending the last vestiges of Gallus' persecution. He was generally a man of high morals who appreciated what was good in Christianity. So many Christians were actually in his service that St Dionysius of Alexandria could say that his palace was almost a church. However, in AD 257 Valerian's policy towards the Christians abruptly changed, a change that seemed connected to the severe trials afflicting the Empire.

The year AD 257 was indeed a bleak one for Rome: plague was continuing to ravage; barbarian tribes were attacking Greece, Asia Minor, crossing the Rhine, sweeping through Hungary and penetrating into northern Italy all at the same time; and the Persians were still relishing their burning of Antioch in AD 256. Valerian met these challenges head on, with him and his son Gallienus leading armies to expel both the barbarians and Persians east and west. The economic cost of fighting these battles and rebuilding Antioch was staggering, emptying the imperial coffers. Taxes, already confiscatory, rose further, while inflation skyrocketed causing a ninety-eight percent drop in the value of Roman currency.

While under these pressures, Valerian began to listen to the whispers of highly placed enemies of the Christians, especially the magician and general Macrianus, that they were secret traitors who hoarded vast amounts of wealth that could be used for the Empire's survival. The Christians were therefore an alien element, whose organization, the Church, must be crushed and its wealth confiscated for the sake of imperial defense. Christianity also provoked the old gods, and the disasters that afflicted Rome were signs of their wrath. So, in the mid summer of AD 257 Valerian issued his first persecuting edict, ordering all bishops to sacrifice to the pagan gods or be exiled. Christians found gathering in cemeteries (i.e., the Catacombs) would be arrested and put to death.

The first bishops sent into exile were St Cyprian of Carthage and St Dionysius of Alexandria. Pope St Stephen died at this time, perhaps while leaving Rome in bad health. Nevertheless, the exiled bishops continued to govern their sees in absentia and the Roman clergy immediately elected Pope Sixtus II as St Stephen's successor. Valerian's edict was not having the desired effect, so he issued a second one commanding all bishops, priests, deacons and Christians belonging to the aristocracy to abjure their faith under penalty of decapitation and loss of goods.

Some of the greatest names enrolled in the Roman martyrology perished during Valerian's persecution: Pope Sixtus II and six of his deacons who were arrested while saying Mass in the Catacombs and immediately beheaded; the deacon Lawrence who was roasted to death on a gridiron; the priests and deacons, together with their entire congregation, who were buried alive by soldiers under an avalanche of stones and sand during Mass near the tomb of Sts Chrysanthus and Daria; the youthful deacon Tarcisius, who was beaten to death while carrying the Eucharist to the home of a Christian; St Cyprian of Carthage, who was recalled from exile and beheaded while kneeling in silent prayer; Bishop Fructuosus of Tarragona and his two deacons, the first martyrs of Spain, burnt to death in witness to Christ.

Like the Decian persecution before it, the Valerian persecution would come to a sudden end due to political catastrophe. Renewed Persian military pressure summoned Valerian once more to the east in AD 260. His campaign at a stalemate, Valerian would seek a negotiated settlement, only to pay a severe price no other Emperor ever suffered:

> "The aging Valerian wore out the plague-thinned ranks of his army marching to and fro against them. Finally, camped before Christian Edessa, he entered into peace negotiations with the formidable and ruthless King Shapur I of Persia, who demanded a personal interview. Valerian came with only a small guard. He was seized and carried off a prisoner to Persia, never to return. It was the first time in history that a Roman emperor had been captured by the enemies of Rome. For five years or more Valerian lived in the utmost degradation, loaded with chains, dressed in his robes of imperial purple for constant mockery; Shapur mounted his horse by placing his feet on Valerian's neck, and when the former emperor finally

died, disgraced and forgotten at Rome, his skin was stuffed with straw and hung up in a Persian temple."[1]

The new Emperor was Valerian's son, Gallienus. One of his first acts was to end the persecution outright, and restore the Church's right both to property and existence. The "Peace of Gallienus", as it became known, gave the Christians freedom of religion and full rights as citizens, and in effect amounted to a restoration of the policy of Alexander Severus. However, in other respects the eight years of Gallienus' reign were extremely perilous as the whole structure of the Empire came close to collapse. Barbarian incursions continued, with three hundred and twenty thousand invading Greece in AD 268 and two hundred and fifty thousand descending into Italy the following year. Rivals seized various provinces and proclaimed independence: the Gallo-Roman Empire comprising Gaul and Britain in the west; the Kingdom of Palmyra comprising Egypt, Syria, Palestine, Armenia in the east. The Juthungi barbarians were now occupying northern Italy and the Vandals were preparing to invade Pannonia. The treasury was again empty and the monetary system in ruins.

The man who would emerge to meet the continuing crisis was Aurelian. He plotted the downfall and death of Gallienus and had Claudius II put in his stead. But his reign would last only two years, with Claudius dying of plague after winning a great victory over the Goths and Heruli in AD 270. The army then proclaimed Aurelian as the new Emperor. In his reign of five years, Aurelian determined to do whatever was necessary to restore the material and moral unity of the Empire. With only his Danubian legions, he stabilized the west, destroyed the rebel state of Palmyra in the east and returned to Rome in triumph as the "restorer of the world" (*restitutor orbis*). At the same time, imperial administration was re-organized, the finances placed on a sound footing, and the monetary system revised. Aurelian also began construction of the now famous wall of defense around the city of Rome, twelve miles long, twenty feet high and twelve feet wide.

With peace restored and the provinces stabilized, Aurelian felt secure enough to construct and implement a new religious policy, and prepared decrees to initiate another persecution of the Christians. The

---

[1] Warren H. Carroll, *The Founding of Christendom* (A History of Christendom), Vol. 1, Christendom Press, 1985, p. 499.

Empire would be united under the worship of the invincible sun (*Solis Invicti*) as the supreme god. Aurelian grieved at the growth of Christianity and attributed its rise to the decline of the old religion. He even once reproached the Roman Senate for not consulting the Sibylline Books in an hour of peril stating, "It would seem as if you were holding your meetings in a church of the Christians instead of a temple of all the gods." In the summer of AD 275, the Edict of Gallienus was rescinded and directives issued to the provincial governors to commence a systematic persecution. However, providentially no official martyrdoms would occur, for before his edict could be executed Aurelian would go the way of so many other Emperors of the third century, being murdered by his own officers.

Themes for study:
- The crises leading to the Valerian persecution.
- The martyrs of the Valerian persecution.
- Aurelian as "restorer of the world."
- Aurelian's failed attempt to renew the persecution.

Further reading:
- *The Catholic Encyclopaedia* (1911, vol. II, p. 108).
- Anne W. Carroll, *Christ the King: Lord of History*, 2nd Ed., Trinity Communications, 1986, p. 95.
- Warren H. Carroll, *The Founding of Christendom* (A History of Christendom), Vol. 1, Christendom Press, 1985, pp. 495-500.
- Fr John Laux, *Church History*, TAN Books and Publishers, 1930, pp. 70-72.

AD 301 to AD 400: THE TRIUMPH OF THE CROSS AND OF ORTHODOXY

The Diocletian Persecution

In the ten years after Aurelian's assassination, five Emperors followed in quick succession: Tacitus, Probus, Carus, Numerian and Carinus. Of these, the last four were also murdered in office. In AD 284, an Illyrian officer named Diocles emerged to take the purple as sole ruler of Rome. As Emperor, he changed his name to Diocletian.

Diocletian was a levelheaded and reflective man who possessed a profound loyalty to the traditions and institutions of the Empire. He clearly saw that the decades of Emperor-killing could not continue if the Empire was to survive. Another system was needed to ensure that the whole Empire could be safely governed without overburdening one man and making him a vulnerable target for the ambitious. Diocletian would share power in a divided Empire. During his first nine years the division would be between two; in AD 293 Diocletian decided that an imperial college of four (the Tetrarchy) would instead govern the Empire: two Augusti and two Caesars. One Augusti would govern the eastern Greek-speaking half of the Empire (including Illyria), and the other Augusti the western half, including Rome. Of the two Augustii, the eastern one held pre-eminence. If ever he was to die or resign the Augusti of the West was required to also resign. Each Augusti would have under him a Caesar who was his designated successor with real power. Each of the four rulers would have their own capital – Nicomedia, Milan, Treves and Sirmium.

Diocletian chose to be Augusti of the more powerful and populous East and appointed as his Caesar another Illyrian of giant physique named Galerius. For the western half, Diocletian appointed two further Illyrians, as Augusti an old comrade-in-arms named Maximian and as his Caesar the calm and gentle Constantius Chlorus. While Diocletian remained at the helm, the Tetrarchy governed well, stabilizing the Empire politically, administratively and economically. It seemed that the great troubles and dangers were now past and the Empire could emerge from its decline.

Religiously, Diocletian was a syncretist who had some knowledge and perhaps sympathy for Christianity. His wife and daughter were probably even catechumens; his entourage comprised many Christians. After the end of Aurelian's plans for persecution, the Church remained undisturbed and very little is heard from her for the whole last quarter of the century. Of the three Popes who reigned from AD 275 to 304 (Eutychian, Caius and Marcellinus), virtually nothing is known of them. Meanwhile, churches were now springing up above ground (more than forty alone in Rome); Bishops were being accorded public honors; Christians were rising to posts in the administration. The only challenge to Christianity came from the pen of the Neo-Platonic philosopher Porphyry of Tyre, who took time to study the teachings of the Church and composed a massive fifteen-volume work against them. It is also important to add, though, that as with previous periods of peace there was a relaxation in the fervor of Christian life.

Of the four Tetrarchs, only Galerius and Maximian possessed any of the old pagan hostility towards Christianity. Galerius received his hostility from his mother Romula, a priestess of the orgiastic mountain gods of Germany. Romula prevailed upon her son to demand a renewal of the persecution against Christianity from Diocletian. At the beginning of AD 303, Galerius approached the senior Emperor at his palace in Nicomedia in Asia Minor with a list of alleged provocations committed by Christians that were disturbing various generals, such as Christian soldiers and officers refusing to sacrifice to pagan gods, or Christians refusing military service *per se*. Diocletian hesitated, refusing to order any action against Christians for six weeks. Eventually, Diocletian gave way to Galerius, issuing on 23 February AD 303 an edict decreeing the removal of all Christians from public office, closing the courts to them, prohibiting the freeing of Christian slaves, and ordering the destruction of all Christian churches and books. That same day, the church in Nicomedia was promptly burnt to the ground. At this point, however, Diocletian held back from ordering the death of any person simply for being a Christian.

It was not long, though, before the persecution was widened in scope. Within a month after the persecution began, two fires were lit in Diocletian's palace in Nicomedia. Paranoid, Diocletian blamed the Christians. All Christians found within the Emperor's palace staff were forced to sacrifice to the pagan gods, including Diocletian's wife and daughter. Those who refused were tortured and killed. The bishop of Nicomedia, Anthimus, was beheaded, together with many others of his flock. About the same time, insurrections broke out in Armenia and Syria, for which the Christians were also blamed. There followed two further decrees, ordering the imprisonment of all Christian clergy who refused to sacrifice. As with past persecutions, many of the clergy apostatized under duress, even Pope Marcellinus handed over copies of the scriptures to the persecutors.[1] But throughout the Empire there were also great martyrs and confessors: Bishop Cyril of Antioch; Bishop Ossius of Cordoba; Bishop Felix of Thibiuca; the deacon Zachaeus; the lectors Procopius and Alphaeus; Sebastian; Catherine; Margaret, etc. There was relative peace for the Christians only in Gaul and Britain, which escaped the full effects of the persecution under Constantius.

During AD 303, Diocletian began the twentieth year of his imperial reign. He was the first Emperor in over 150 years to achieve this milestone. But within a month after attending grueling celebrations in Rome, Diocletian underwent a sudden and deep psychological collapse that left him totally incapacitated. Perhaps his conscience had caught up with him, or his superstitious mind was dwelling on what had happened to previous great persecutors of Christianity: Nero, Domitian, Decius and Valerian. For the remainder of the year and for the whole of AD 304 Diocletian was unseen in public, finally emerging in March AD 305 a pathetic and unrecognizable figure.

The moment had come for Galerius to fill the void. For all intents and purposes he now ruled the eastern Empire without restraint. Goaded on by his mother, Galerius issued another decree against the Christians in the spring of AD 304: all Christians, regardless of office, sex or age were to

---

[1] Those who handed over the sacred books were called by their more uncompromising brethren *Traditores*, from whence English derives the modern word 'traitor.'

sacrifice to the pagan gods or die. A new wave of celebrated martyrdoms now flowed: Bishop Philip of Heraclea; the priest Saturninus of Carthage, and fifty members of his congregation; the entire population of one whole town in Phrygia; the sisters Agape, Irene and Chione.

AD 304 would prove to be one of the most frightful in the history of the ten great persecutions. Countless numbers of Christians were martyred throughout the whole Empire, mainly in the East: Asia Minor; Palestine; Phoenicia; Syria; North Africa; Macedonia; Thrace; Illyricum; Rhaetia; and Italy. Probably the worst of the persecution was inflicted upon the Christians of Egypt. Eusebius provides a dramatic eyewitness account of the shocking mutilations inflicted upon as many as one hundred Christians per day, including women and children.[2] This massacre continued on a daily basis for almost a year. The same historian also details the massacres of Christians in his native province in a whole book entitled, *The History of the Martyrs of Palestine*. Constantine the Great, as Emperor, would later comment that if Diocletian had slain as many barbarians as he had slaughtered Christians there would have been no barbarians remaining to threaten the Empire. The Acts of the Martyrs from this period record the names of many child martyrs and their ages – Agnes, Lucy, Eulalia, Justus, Pastor, Maxima, Secunda, Domitilla, all between the ages of nine and fourteen. On the other hand, Rome faired relatively well, with few martyrdoms and the Pope remaining undisturbed, suggesting that Pope Marcellinus may have purchased immunity for himself and his flock from local officials.

By the end of AD 304, Pope Marcellinus was dead, dying of natural causes. The Papal See would remain vacant for the next two years due to the persecution and internal divisions. The martyrdoms continued unabated, as did Galerius' determination to destroy the Church. Nor was Galerius intent on lessening his grip on power, even after Diocletian's re-emergence in March AD 305. Galerius virtually ordered Diocletian to abdicate as Augusti, but this only opened another complication for the ambitious tyrant. Diocletian's abdication would automatically result in Maximian's abdication as Augusti in the West, allowing Constantius with his Christian sympathies to assume the predominant position of power in Rome. In addition, Constantius' son, the highly popular Constantine,

---

[2] Eusebius, *The History of the Church*, 8, 9.

would assume the position of Caesar. Though still a pagan, Constantine's sympathies for Christianity were growing, particularly as his mother Helena professed faith in Christ. Galerius agreed to the accession of Constantius as Augusti, but insisted on appointing his Caesar, namely his nephew Daia, thus deliberately excluding Constantine.

Themes for study:
- The division of the Empire according to the system of four Tetrarchs.
- Galerius Caesar as the real instigator of the Great Persecution.
- The escalation of the persecution through successive decrees.
- Diocletian's psychological collapse and disappearance from public life.

Further reading:
- Warren H. Carroll, *The Founding of Christendom* (A History of Christendom), Vol. 1, Christendom Press, 1985, pp. 501-508.
- Fernard Hayward, *A History of the Popes*, J.M. Dent & Sons Ltd., 1931, pp. 37-38.
- Philip Hughes, *A History of the Church*, Vol. 1, Sheed and Ward, 1948, pp. 168-172.
- Fr John Laux, *Church History*, TAN Books and Publishers, 1930, pp. 73-74.

The Ascendancy of Constantine

With the resignation of Diocletian and Maximian in AD 305, Galerius and his new Caesar, his nephew Daia, intensified the persecution of Christianity still further. The next edict issued in AD 306 was akin to Decius': it required all citizens, not merely those suspected of Christianity, to sacrifice. New horrors were devised by gross magistrates not just interested in enforcing State policy, but also looking to indulge in looting and lust. The martyrdom of Ulpian of Tyre was one example of the horror: he was thrown into the sea inside an ox-skin with a rabid dog and poisonous viper.

At the same time, Galerius and Daia began to implement their scheme for reforming Paganism throughout the Empire. Paganism itself would become a "church", with restored and new temples, a hierarchical priesthood headed by a high priest in each province and a standardized liturgy. Prominent 'magicians' of Paganism would also be appointed to important governmental posts. Anti-Christian propaganda was reproduced and spread throughout the cities and countryside. Galerius' efforts would reap some success, and he took delight at hearing news that attendances at Pagan services were rising again. It was, therefore, in the interest of this new 'church' that the persecution be continued.

However, in the West the situation was changing. While Maximian ruled as Augusti in Italy, Spain and Africa the persecution raged as in the East; but where Constantius Chlorus ruled as Caesar, in Britain and in Gaul, there was virtually no persecution at all. After Constantius became Augusti, Spain passed to him and there the persecution ceased. His Caesar, Maxentius, ruled Africa and Italy, and likewise did not enforce the persecuting decrees.

Meanwhile, Constantius' son, Constantine, was a virtual prisoner of Galerius in his palace in Nicomedia. Galerius had prevented his elevation into the Tetrarchy and intended to permanently keep him out. While in Nicomedia, Constantine was sixteen hundred miles away from his father and the support of his Legions. Galerius may well have been contemplating his murder, while Constantine considered options for escaping. The opportunity came when a sick Constantius wrote Galerius requesting that his son be allowed to join him to deal with the barbarian Picts attacking his troops in Britain. Galerius hesitated, but one night while drunk he gave Constantine permission to depart. When Galerius woke up the following day at noon, Constantine was already fifty miles away and crossing the Bosphorus.

In July AD 306 Constantius died at York in Britain. Galerius maneuvered to have him replaced by another favorable to his policy of persecution, namely, Flavius Severus. In this he was thwarted. Maxentius, the son of Maximian, took over Rome on promises of restoring its old-time privileges as the imperial capital. Once secure, he established a corrupt and licentious tyranny. Meanwhile, in a dramatic move the Legions in Britain enthusiastically gave their support to Constantine, who had successfully crossed the English Channel, to be his father's successor. This coup d'etat was a serious setback to Galerius and his plans for a universal 'Pagan Church.'

The years AD 307 and 308 were to be politically chaotic ones. Galerius did not recognize the elevation of Maxentius and Constantine and launched a campaign to recapture the West. However, in successive battles Severus was killed and Galerius was expelled from Italy. Even Maximian attempted a comeback, only to be driven out of Rome by his own son. Desperate, Galerius sought the help of Diocletian and called him out of retirement to attend a conference aimed at putting together a coalition against Maxentius (it was reported that Diocletian was loathed to leave his cabbage farm). Throughout all this, Constantine remained aloof and did not participate.

Religiously, the years AD 307 and 308 witnessed a moderate decline in the level of persecution, except in Egypt where it continued unabated. A new Pope in Rome was finally elected, Marcellus, who undertook without delay the reorganization of public worship in temporary buildings. Soon after, a riot was raised against Marcellus by disaffected Christians who thought that his penances for the lapsed were too extreme. He was exiled by order of Maxentius and not long after died. His successor, Eusebius, suffered virtually the same fate, this time forced into exile in Sicily by rigorists who believed that the lapsed should never be forgiven. Galerius remained resolved to destroy Christianity and renewed full-scale persecution in the East in AD 309. This renewal brought about significant martyrdoms in Christian Edessa and Palestine, including the scholar Pamphilus.

In AD 310 the political ground began to move once again. Maximian continued to intrigue and was executed by Constantine after a failed assassination attempt. When Diocletian heard of his old partner's death he wept and raved, and began to starve himself to death. As Diocletian began to die, likewise Galerius. A huge ulcer, the result of venereal disease, began to eat away at his body, producing a foul smell that filled every room he entered. Facing a ghastly death, Galerius began to whimper and fear the vengeance of the Christian God. On 30 April AD 311, Galerius issued a decree ending the persecution of Christianity (while at the same time continuing to insult it). Admitting defeat, the decree asked the Christians to pray that their God will turn away His wrath from him. The joy of the Christians knew no bounds. Six days later, Galerius was dead.

Themes for study:
- The further escalation of persecution by Galerius and Daia.
- The political chaos of the years AD 307-308.
- Constantine's coup d'etat in the West.
- Galerius' decree ending the persecution and his subsequent death.

Further reading:
- Warren H. Carroll, *The Founding of Christendom* (A History of Christendom), Vol. 1, Christendom Press, 1985, pp. 508-513.
- Fernard Hayward, *A History of the Popes*, J.M. Dent & Sons Ltd., 1931, pp. 38-39.
- Philip Hughes, *A History of the Church*, Vol. 1, Sheed and Ward, 1948, pp. 172-173.
- Fr John Laux, *Church History*, TAN Books and Publishers, 1930, pp. 74-75.

The Triumph of Constantine

After the death of Galerius, four rulers jostled between themselves for control of various parts of the Empire: Constantine and Maxentius in the West; Licinius and Maximin Daia in the East. Rivalry and jealousy between the Tetrarchs was growing and secret negotiations were being conducted between Maxentius and Maximin in preparation for war against Constantine and Licinius. On hearing that the alliance between Maxentius and Maximin was signed and sealed Constantine decided to strike first.

Constantine's plan was to strike at Maxentius' territories in Rhaetia and Italy before Maximin could come to his aid from the East. Constantine could trust Licinius as an ally, for his sister Constantia was engaged to marry him. Constantine could also present himself as a liberator of the people of Rome who were suffering under the excesses of the licentious Maxentius; and in the eyes of the Christians, Constantine would be favored by those who could remember his father's refusal to enforce the persecuting decrees of Diocletian and Galerius.

At the beginning of AD 312, Constantine and his army were on the Rhine frontier guarding against barbarian incursions. At a council of war in his winter base in Alsace, thoughts of marching on Rome were greeted with skepticism and even opposition from Constantine's generals. Recent expeditions by Severus and Galerius had ended disastrously. The supply lines would be dangerously long and Constantine lacked numerical superiority. Constantine consulted the gods, and through their haruspices his planned adventure was condemned. Meanwhile, Maxentius was enlarging his army with conscripts from Africa, Sicily and Italy to one hundred thousand men, and strengthening its most potent element, the cataphracti, or armored cavalry. His plan was to march northwards into Rhaetia and then strike westwards deep into Gaul against Constantine.

Despite the doubts, Constantine determined to seize the advantage with a surprise attack. Assembling a force of only forty thousand men, Constantine crossed the Alps and was in northern Italy before Maxentius was aware of anything. When hearing that Constantine was outside the city of Susa he had to abandon all thought of an offensive and hurriedly planned a defense of his own territory. Constantine burned down the gates of Susa and slaughtered all the enemy troops. Turin was an even greater disaster for Maxentius, whose fine army in battle array was slaughtered outside the walls of the city. Turin then opened its gates to the conqueror Constantine, as next did Milan. Moving eastwards, Constantine then won successive battles at Brescia and Verona, completing the rout of Maxentius' forces in the north. With the territory to his rear now secure, Constantine could move south on Rome.

At this time, Constantine was still officially a pagan, still consulting the haruspices and carrying out the external ceremonies of the State religion. Yet, he had been and was still receiving influences from various sources, including his father Constantius who had adopted the monotheism of the god Sol and his mother Helena who had embraced Christianity. Constantine had also witnessed the bravery and resistance of the Christians in the face of persecution and this caused him to realize that they were a powerful force in both religion and politics. His practical sense could also appreciate that while the great persecutors of Christianity, Diocletian and Galerius, had respectively gone mad and rotted away, his father Constantius had spared the Christians and avoided a miserable end. Maybe the God of the Christians would also come to his aid as he approached Rome?

The historian Eusebius in his *Life of Constantine* (1:27-30) relates what happened next, according to Constantine's own personal testimony given to him under oath twenty years after the event: It was while on march in Gaul months before the final battle that Constantine felt the need of divine assistance and began to consider "in which God he ought to put his trust." Reflecting on the wretched end of the persecuting rulers, Constantine prayed to the God of his father Constantius. Then came the miraculous portent. As the sun was descending, Constantine saw in the sky "a trophy in the shape of a dazzling cross in front of the sun and with it a motto saying 'With this sign thou shalt conquer'" (*In Hoc Signo Vinces*). Constantine and all his army saw the sign and were struck in wonder. That same night, "while he slept there appeared to him Christ of God with the sign he had seen in the sky, who told him to make standards of that shape to serve as a protection in his conflicts with the enemy." Lactantius, in his work *The Deaths of the Persecutors* (44), adds that on the night before the battle outside Rome "Constantine was warned in his sleep to mark on the shields of his men the heavenly sign of God and thus go to battle; he did as he was commanded and putting the letter X on its side turned back the top arm thus making the name of Christ."

Why did God choose Constantine in so critical a time for Rome and Christianity? Many have pointed out his unworthiness, hesitancy, errors and even crimes, criticisms that in large part are justified. Nevertheless, the Holy Spirit, like the wind, blows where it will, and more often than not works through human instruments who are at best imperfect in His eyes and even ours. Constantine was chosen because he was the most able man available in the highest position at the time to initiate the task of founding Christendom; and God knew that he was disposed enough to listen to His voice and conquer in His sign.

As Constantine marched down the *Via Flaminia* towards Rome, Maxentius began to panic and lose all sense of strategy. He locked himself in his own palace fearing to go out for the haruspices had warned him that if he left the city gates he would die. Hearing that local Romans were crying out in favor of Constantine, Maxentius panicked further and sought counsel from the Sibylline Books. The reply was that "the enemy of the Romans would die that very day." Thinking that the prophecy meant Constantine, Maxentius was encouraged and left the city to take his place in front of his army drawn up for battle.

The site of the battle was Saxa Rubra (Red Rocks) nine miles outside of Rome on the Tiber River. Maxentius had positioned himself to bar any further advance by Constantine on Rome. His strongest and most loyal troops were his Praetorians and the cataphracti. They were positioned in the center, while the weak and unreliable mercenaries were stationed on the flanks. The battle opened with Constantine personally leading the attack on the enemy's center. The fighting was initially fierce and difficult. Eventually, the cataphracti were dispersed with the blows of heavy maces; the Praetorians fought bravely to the last man. Seeing the rout of their powerful cavalry and best troops, the mercenary infantry turned and fled towards Rome. Chaos now reigned as thousands of fleeing troops sought to reach Rome over two bridges crossing the Tiber — the Milvian Bridge and a hastily prepared wooden pontoon bridge. Under the weight of thousands of armored troops, the pontoon bridge collapsed, dropping those on it into the river that was then swollen by the autumn rains.

One of the fugitives was Maxentius. He had managed to get within reach of the opposite bank, but fell back into the mud and drowned due to his heavy armor. The next day his body was found, his head cut off and stuck to the end of a pike, on which it was carried in triumph by Constantine's soldiers to Rome. With the bulk of Maxentius' fleeing army cut off or destroyed, the way was open to the Eternal City, whose gates at this time were being opened to receive its new Augusti. It was 28 October AD 312.

The next day, 29 October, Constantine triumphantly entered Rome. He was received with joy by enormous crowds of Pagans and Christians, including Senators and public officials. He showed himself remarkably merciful in victory. There was to be no major outpouring of revenge and bloodletting, except for the execution of Maxentius' son and other major crime-stained collaborators of the previous tyranny. The memory of Diocletian, Maximian and Galerius was condemned and their monuments destroyed. A statue of Constantine was erected in his honor and the construction of a triumphal arch was voted for.

Constantine would not disappoint the Christians. He officially attributed his victory to the inspiration of "Divinity" and did not perform the customary pagan sacrifices giving thanks to Jupiter for his victory on Capitoline Hill. In the short number of months he stayed in Rome after his triumph, Constantine worked on solving many problems, including discussing restitution and indemnities to the Roman and African churches with Pope Miltiades. All the property taken from the twenty-five churches of Rome was restored, together with substantial additional donations. For the Africans, Constantine went further, ordering the payment of three thousand double denarii for the support of "certain specified ministers of the lawful and holy Catholic religion" – the first act of State aid for the Church.

Of even greater significance for Christians were the deliberations between Constantine and Licinius in Milan in March AD 313, which resulted in the promulgation of a new law in both the western and eastern parts of the Empire dealing with the question of religion. The Edict of Milan, as it became known, would go further than the Edict of Toleration issued by Galerius two years earlier. There would be no insults of Christianity or a justification of past persecutions; more importantly, it made no mention of Paganism as the official religion of the State. It was more concerned with the rights of subjects of the Empire, guaranteeing full religious liberty to all, Pagan and Christian. The significance of this law cannot be understated: it amounted to the laying of the first permanent foundation stone of a new civilization – one in which Jesus Christ would reign as King.

Themes for study:
- Constantine's decision to war against the tyrant Maxentius.
- The vision, *"In Hoc Signo Vinces"*; and the dream, *"Chi-Rho"*.
- Constantine's victory at the Battle of Milvian Bridge.
- The Edict of Milan, March AD 313.

Further reading:
- Warren H. Carroll, *The Founding of Christendom* (A History of Christendom), Vol. 1, Christendom Press, 1985, pp. 524-532.
- Philip Hughes, *A History of the Church*, Vol. 1, Sheed and Ward, 1948, pp. 175-176.
- Fr John Laux, *Church History*, TAN Books and Publishers, 1930, pp. 76-77.
- Abbot Giuseppe Ricciotti, *The Age of Martyrs – Christianity from Diocletian to Constantine*, TAN Books and Publishers, 1959, pp. 150-177.

The Donatist Heresy

Unnoticed during the course of the Great Persecution of Diocletian, a storm was quietly brewing in the Church of North Africa that would test the newly established religious peace of Constantine. The Church in North Africa had always been characterized by the prevalence of rigorism since the days of Tertullian. Now it was to re-emerge in a new strain known as Donatism.

The rigorists advocated the view that any bishop who had collaborated with the Roman authorities during the Great Persecution was by that very fact permanently excommunicated and deprived of ecclesiastical office. When the moderate Caecilian was consecrated Bishop of Carthage in AD 312, the rigorists objected, citing that at least one of his episcopal consecrators (Felix of Aptunga) had collaborated with the persecutors and therefore was no longer capable of administering the sacraments validly. The rigorist bishops of Numidia proceeded to elevate one of their own party, Majorinus, as bishop, thus affecting a formal schism. When Majorinus died after only one year in office he was replaced by Donatus (from whence is derived the name for this schism and heresy).

Donatus, like most heretics, was an able but proud man. Both he and his followers were noted for their obnoxious temperament, malevolence and hypocrisy. Two principal Donatist Bishops, Silvanus of Cirta and Purpurius of Limata, were later found to be respectively guilty of theft, embezzlement, simony and murder. Constantine at first clearly backed the Caecilian party, intending to restore confiscated property to them. The Donatists appealed, asking Constantine in a letter dated 5 April AD 313 to appoint three bishops from Gaul (where there had been no persecution and hence no collaborators) to arbitrate the dispute. Constantine, knowing well the structure of the Church, referred the matter to Pope Miltiades, who set up a council of fifteen Italian bishops plus the three requested by the Donatists from Gaul.

This Council met in Rome for three days in October AD 313. Pope Miltiades, himself from Africa, presided, while Caecilian and Donatus were both on hand to present their cases personally. Each was also allowed to have present ten bishops of their own persuasion from North Africa. The sum of the evidence put forward by both sides weighed in favor of Caecilian, while Donatus was exposed as a heretic for rebaptizing those who had joined his faction and reconsecrating bishops who had done likewise. Donatus was condemned, and he and his followers were ordered to submit to Caecilian. Donatus would have none of this and accused the Council of having been stacked, demanding at the same time that his case be tried only by the bishops of Gaul. He then proceeded to again appeal to Constantine, attaching favorable reports about the Donatists from the Governors of Africa.

Fearing the scandal that would be caused by the continuing public quarrel between Christians, as well as the civil disruption to the Empire, Constantine re-opened the matter for investigation, this time before a larger Council of bishops meeting at Arles in Gaul. This decision was made while Pope Miltiades was dying, and when the Council finally met in August AD 314 Silvester I was sitting in the throne of St Peter. Comprising forty-six bishops from Constantine's dominions and Legates sent by Pope Sylvester, the Council declared the consecration of Caecilian to be valid, confirmed the decision of the Council of Rome and excommunicated all those who obstinately adhered to Donatus and his schism.

The Council canons were then submitted to Pope Sylvester for his approval, while the Donatists again appealed to Constantine who exclaimed, "O insolent madness! They appeal from heaven to earth, and from Jesus Christ to a man." In a written response, Constantine upheld the rulings of the Councils of Rome and Arles in November AD 316, and in March AD 317 sent soldiers to enforce (with the spilling of much blood) the return of Donatist churches to the Catholics. Despite further efforts by Constantine to effect a reconciliation between AD 317 and 321, the Donatists remained recalcitrant, and continued to be a powerful and at times violent force in North Africa for more than another century, having their center around the stolen cathedral of Cirta.[1] St Optatus of Milevis wrote an extensive work against them in the AD 360's. Favored briefly by the Emperor Julian the Apostate, the schism substantially waned after another condemnation by the Council of Carthage in AD 411. It would be the great St Augustine of Hippo who finally developed the

---

[1] The Donatists had marauding bands known as the *Circumcellions*, which fell upon Catholics mutilating and murdering them with the battle cry, "Praise the Lord!"

theology that the true minister of the sacraments is Christ and thus the unworthiness of any human minister does not affect their efficacy.

Other matters occupied the mind of Constantine during these exacting times that would eventually and permanently transform the whole fabric of the Empire. The task of transforming the Empire's thousand-year pagan structure of life and law was begun in AD 315 by a series of decrees aimed at making it, over time, fully Christian. The following persons were now protected from torture, killing or cruelty: wives, children, foundlings, slaves, tenants, convicts, prisoners of war. Christians were encouraged to free slaves with a priest as witness. Slave families were no longer to be separated when being sold or dividing inheritance. The old Augustan laws against celibacy were abolished; likewise prostitution in public taverns. Crucifixion, facial branding and gladiatorial contests were also abolished. The most important public offices were now being entrusted to Christians. Construction was begun on magnificent churches such as St Peter's, St Paul's-outside-the-Walls and St John Lateran's. Sunday was designated by law a day of rest for all. This last enactment would remain a corner stone of western civilization for the next seventeen centuries.

However, to bring about the full establishment of a Christian Roman Empire, the division between East and West, together with Licinius himself, had to be disposed of. Since being appointed by Galerius, Licinius had displayed nothing but the old Roman love of the sword and power and contempt for Christianity. During a brief war in AD 314 caused by Licinius' plotting to destabilize his so-called partner, Constantine had wrested from him most of eastern Europe, except Thrace. Brooding over his losses, Licinius sought revenge and targeted those within his realm whom he thought were sympathetic to Constantine, namely the Christians. Beginning in AD 319, Licinius first prohibited Christian bishops from meeting in synod; then forbade Christian men and women meeting together in public and for private instruction on the pretext that such gatherings promoted immorality. Soon, all Christians in the army and in government were ordered to sacrifice to the gods or be dismissed from office; and finally, bishops were ordered to sacrifice or face execution. It was a return to the darkest hours of the Diocletian persecution. The most famous martyrs of this persecution were the forty soldiers of the Twelfth Legion of Sebaste, who rather than sacrifice chose to die standing together naked in a freezing ice pond at night in the sight of heated baths.

In AD 323, Constantine, hearing the cry of the afflicted eastern Christians, invaded Thrace with one hundred and thirty thousand men. Marching again under the Labarum and with the battle cry *Deus Sumus Salvator!* (God the Supreme Savior!), Constantine routed Licinius in successive battles at Hadrianople and Byzantium. Constantine pursued Licinius into Asia Minor, retracing the road he had traveled on eighteen years earlier as an escapee from the clutches of Galerius. Licinius was again defeated at Chrysopolis, forcing him to surrender to Constantine at Nicomedia. A few months later, Licinius was executed. Constantine was now the sole master of the Roman world.

Constantine knew it was not by his own strength that he had assumed the most powerful civil position in the world, and accordingly gave thanks to God:

> "And from the West, believing that this gift had been entrusted to myself, I have come to the East which was in sorer need of my aid. At the same time I am absolutely persuaded that I owe my whole life, my every breath, and in a word my most secret thoughts to the supreme God."

Themes for study:
- The rise and nature of the Donatist heresy.
- The Councils of Rome and Arles.
- Constantine's laws transforming Roman society.
- Constantine as the master of the whole Roman world.

Further reading:
- Warren H. Carroll, *The Founding of Christendom* (A History of Christendom), Vol. 1, Christendom Press, 1985, pp. 532-543.
- Fernard Hayward, *A History of the Popes*, J.M. Dent & Sons Ltd., 1931, pp. 39-42.
- Fr John Laux, *Church History*, TAN Books and Publishers, 1930, pp. 147-149.
- Abbot Giuseppe Ricciotti, *The Age of Martyrs – Christianity from Diocletian to Constantine*, TAN Books and Publishers, 1959, pp. 228-246.

Arianism and the Council of Nicaea

As the tumult over the Donatist controversy continued, another and more virulent heresy was about to explode out from Egypt and consume the entire East. Unlike most other heresies of the preceding century, this one was unconnected with rigorism, but instead concerned the very person of Christ. It was soon to become known as Arianism, after its greatest proponent, Arius, a priest of Alexandria.

During the last decades of the third century, Lucian of Antioch began teaching the inferiority and subordination of the Son to the Father. Some years later, this teaching was picked up and developed by his disciple Arius. Using the analogy of human fatherhood, Arius taught that as a father always pre-dates his son there was a time when the son was not. Applying this to the Father and the Logos, Arius stated, "God has not always been Father; there was a moment when he was alone, and was not yet Father: later he became so." Christ was therefore not co-eternal and consequently not of the same substance as the Father. Rather, He was only a creature and son of God by virtue of being "like in substance" to the Father. As the created Logos, Christ was free, subject to change and determined to good by his own choice. The Holy Spirit was the first of the creatures created by Him.

Arianism was to sweep across the Christian world as a whirlwind, catching all virtually by surprise. As St Jerome later declared, "The world awoke and found itself Arian." One reason for its rapid success was Arius himself. He was tall, distinguished and polished. Women were charmed by his appearance, manners and aura of holiness. Men were impressed with his intellectual prowess and preaching ability.

Arius' first great opponent was the Bishop of Alexandria, St Alexander. In private and public debates between the Catholics and Arians, he came to understand the Arian doctrines in full. After enquiry and consultation, he called upon Arius to abandon his beliefs. Arius refused, and thereupon St Alexander proceeded to excommunicate him and all his followers. The Bishop then wrote to most of the eastern

Bishops (more than seventy letters in all), as well as to Pope Silvester, warning them of this heresy that reduced Christ to the level of a mere creature.

Arius likewise began a letter writing campaign "to all the bishops", and traveled northwards to Asia Minor to take up refuge with his powerful friend Eusebius, Bishop of Nicomedia. Arius also had the clear support of the other Eusebius, the historian. Emboldened, Arius organized a body of supporters and distributed letters, pamphlets and popular songs (*Thalia*) embodying his doctrine. Bishop Alexander responded in kind, and the East was soon split by the controversy – the bishops of Egypt siding with Bishop Alexander; those of Asia Minor with Arius.

A crisis situation rapidly developed in Antioch in December AD 324 after the death of its Bishop Philogonius. Rival Catholic and Arian supporters began rioting in the streets over his successor, preventing any election from occurring. Constantine, aware of the growing controversy, sent his own ecclesiastical adviser, Bishop Ossius of Cordoba, to Egypt to affect a resolution. He organized a synod of more than fifty bishops from all over the East that met during the Easter of AD 325. The synod chose the staunch Catholic, Eustathius of Beroea, as the new Bishop of Antioch and condemned Arian bishops for heresy. It was also determined that a "great and holy council" should gather to deal with the whole question of Arianism.

The idea for an ecumenical council was probably first mooted by Bishop Ossius to Constantine, who decided that it should convene at Nicaea in Bithynia. Bishop Ossius would actively preside over the Council's deliberations in the presence of the Emperor who was honorary president (Constantine termed himself "external bishop", though he understood little about the controversy). Two priests from Rome, Vitus and Vincent, were sent as representatives of Pope Silvester, who was unable to attend personally due to age. The Council commenced on 20 May AD 325 with a splendid ceremonial and a welcoming address given by Bishop Eusebius of Nicomedia. Present were 250 bishops, mainly from the eastern half of the Empire; before the Council's conclusion the number would grow to 318. Eleven came from Greece, and one each from Spain, Gaul and Africa. Bishops were also present from outside the Empire, including Armenia and Persia. Twenty-two bishops specifically came as supporters of Arius.[1]

Constantine opened the first session of discussions with a discourse: "I consider dissension in the Church more dreadful and more painful than any other war ... when I heard of your dissensions, I was convinced that this matter required my attention before all others, and therefore, in the hope of being some service to you, I called you together to this meeting." During the course of formal deliberations only one bishop could speak at a time, followed by debate. However, in private conferences and semi-public disputations St Alexander's young archdeacon, the thirty-year-old St Athanasius, shone as the champion of orthodoxy, exposing as blasphemous statements of the elderly Arius. An Arian profession of faith drafted by Eusebius of Nicomedia was presented and read. The vast majority of bishops rose up in indignation against it, provoked by the endless subterfuges of Arius' faction. It soon became impossible for anyone to defend the heretic, and most of his supporters abandoned all open support.

What was more difficult was the drafting of a creedal statement that was unequivocally Catholic and beyond any manipulation by the Arians. Bishop Ossius put forward a term to describe Christ he knew to be objectionable to the Arians, *homo-ousios*, that is, "one in being" with the Father. However, many orthodox bishops also disliked this term as it was not found in Scripture and had been used in decades past by the Sabellians to convey the notion that the Father and the Son were the same Person. Nevertheless, the term was identical to Tertullian's *consubstantialis*, and it had long been used in the West in an orthodox sense. Bishop Ossius induced Constantine to call upon the Council Fathers to accept a creed that embodied this term, which was read by the deacon Hermogenes and presented for signature on 19 June AD 325.

All the Bishops, including Eusebius of Nicomedia, signed. Constantine then sent orders to Alexandria to secure acceptance of the Council's decree and the removal of dissenters. Only two Libyans — Theonas of Marmarica and Secundas of Ptolemais — who were supporters

---

[1] Traditionally, there were 318 bishops at the Council, but the final creedal statement bears the signatures of only 220. It is speculated by the Protestant scholar Harnack that there were between 1,700 and 1,800 bishops in the world at the time of the Council.

of Arius from the beginning, refused to put their names to the decree. They found themselves condemned with Arius and exiled to Illyricum. Three months later, Eusebius of Nicomedia and Theognis of Nicaea were also banished for refusing to recognize Arius' condemnation, giving hospitality to Arians, and for openly professing Arian doctrines.

The great Council ended with a brilliant banquet in the imperial palace. Eusebius the historian likened it to "a foreshadowing of Christ's kingdom." With admonitions to peace and concord, Constantine dismissed the bishops to their homes. It was a supreme moment in the Emperor's life. He was the acknowledged protector of the Church and had brought peace to her. In reality, however, it was far too premature to celebrate a final triumph over Arianism.

Themes for study:
- The rise and nature of the Arian heresy: Lucian of Antioch and Arius the Priest.
- The early attempts of St Alexander of Alexandria to crush Arianism.
- Constantine's intervention to resolve the crisis.
- The Council of Nicaea and the creedal statement condemning Arianism.

Further reading:
- Warren H. Carroll, *The Founding of Christendom* (A History of Christendom), Vol. 2, Christendom Press, 1987, pp. 9-12.
- Fernard Hayward, *A History of the Popes*, J.M. Dent & Sons Ltd., 1931, pp. 43-45.
- Philip Hughes, *A History of the Church*, Vol. 1, Sheed and Ward, 1948, pp. 189-193.
- Fr John Laux, *Church History*, TAN Books and Publishers, 1930, pp. 109-112.

The Post-Nicene Struggle

The Arian heresy should have ended with the Council of Nicaea. However, the Council only proved to be a prelude to a struggle that would persist for over the next fifty years. For the first time in the Church's history, not only was a heresy to survive its initial condemnation, but also was to rebound and wreak havoc within and without the Church — all due to a new element in the world, the Christian Emperor.

Immediately after their defeat in the Council, the Arian hardliners began a quiet but determined effort to regain imperial favor with a view to winning ascendancy in the Church. The weak link through which this would be achieved was Constantine's sister and widow of Licinius, Constantia. She had always been an ardent follower of Arius and had Eusebius of Nicomedia as her spiritual adviser. After Eusebius' exile, Constantia took on another Arian priest and recommended him to her brother's special care. Though his name remains a mystery, this priest was a master of manipulation and intrigue and before long had convinced Constantine that Arius, Eusebius and Theognis were no heretics at all but rather victims of personal enmity and envy.

After only three years, Eusebius and Theognis were recalled from exile and reinstated to their old Sees in AD 330. Back comfortably in power and imperial favor, Eusebius began implementing his master plan for revenge over those who had him exiled. Knowing that he could not launch a full frontal attack against Nicaea, Eusebius planned instead to depose one by one those who had supported the term *homo-ousios*, replacing them with bishops who would substitute an Arian formula. The first victim was the staunch Eustathius of Antioch, who was slandered and deposed by an Arian synod as a Sabellian, which then installed the Arian Paulinus of Tyre in his place. Constantine dealt with the riots that followed by exiling Eustathius, who remained in exile until his death in AD 338.

The next target was the new bishop of Alexandria, St Athanasius. The plan was to force him to accept Arius back into Alexandria and restore him to his previous ecclesiastical standing. Eusebius had thought it through thoroughly: Constantine would summon Arius to Constantinople; Arius would submit an ambiguous profession of faith that would be accepted by the Emperor; Arius would then be allowed to return to Alexandria. However, St Athanasius would have none of it, even refusing the express order of the Emperor: "There can be no communion between the Catholic Church and a heresy which fights against Christ." Furious at his stubbornness, the Arians determined to oust St Athanasius whatever the cost.

It began with Eusebius conspiring with local Alexandrian schismatics (the Meletians) to concoct a series of calumnies against the champion of orthodoxy: St Athanasius was sending gold to a political rebel; he had profaned the Precious Blood at an Arian Mass; he was sexually immoral; he practiced magic; he had murdered a bishop by the name of Arsenius and used his dead hand in magic spells. Eusebius demanded a council to investigate the charges, which met at Constantine's order at Antioch, presided over by Constantine's brother. St Athanasius demolished the charges, even producing alive the allegedly murdered bishop.

Unfortunately, St Athanasius' victory was short-lived. Eusebius convinced Constantine to order another council to rehear the same charges at Tyre in AD 335. With St Athanasius came forty-nine Egyptian bishops, who were all refused admission. The jury was already chosen, Arians to a man, with Eusebius at their head. The council president was a carefully selected imperial official. St Athanasius foresaw his condemnation and secretly hastened to Constantinople.

St Athanasius personally confronted Constantine as he entered the city on horseback, grabbing his horse's bridle and demanding a just inquiry into the charges against him. Constantine reluctantly consented, and the Arians were summoned from Tyre. Arriving, they raised a new charge against St Athanasius — that he had conspired to prevent grain shipments from Alexandria to Constantinople. This charge, like all the others, was bogus, but was testified to by a number of schismatic bishops. Convinced and enraged, Constantine exiled St Athanasius to Treves in France (AD 335). The joy of Eusebius was unrestrained, who then proceeded to raise the Arian Pistus to the Alexandrian See. Curiously enough, the Pope at the time, Silvester, made no attempt to actively intervene in these proceedings. This could have been due to his age, or weakness, or more broadly, to the founding of Constantinople by the Emperor, a move that transferred political supremacy emphatically to the

East, leaving Rome feeling abandoned and excluded from political life.

The next step was to have Arius received back into the Church with all due pomp and ceremony. To arrange this in Alexandria was out of the question, for despite the exile of St Athanasius the local people, who were now in a state of continuous rioting, remained firmly behind him. Manipulating Constantine again, Eusebius convinced the Emperor to call Arius to Constantinople and order the local Bishop, Alexander, to restore him into communion with the Church. Alexander refused, praying that either Arius or himself die before such an outrage occur. In Constantinople, too, Arius' arrival divided the city into conflicting factions. The Catholics stormed heaven with prayers to avert the disaster, all apparently in vain for the day was fixed and the church chosen. However, the very day before the event, while walking on his way to see Constantine, Arius' bowels burst open and he fell immediately dead in the presence of friends and onlookers.

Undaunted by the death of the heresiarch, the Arian party forged on. Alexander of Constantinople was to die soon after Arius and was replaced by a Catholic named Paul. He was not to last long, being deposed and an Arian put in his place. The East was rapidly falling to the Arians, with only Egypt remaining steadfastly Catholic. Furthermore, it was by Arian hands, those of Eusebius himself, that Constantine would receive baptism on his deathbed in AD 337.

The successors to Constantine were his sons, Constantine II, Constans and Constantius II. The first two were Catholics while the third was an outright Arian. Constantine II was given Spain, Gaul and Britain to govern; Constans received Africa, Italy, Dacia and Macedonia; while Thrace, Asia, Pontus and Egypt fell to Constantius II. The struggle for orthodoxy would be re-ignited under them in AD 340 by Constantine II's decision to permit St Athanasius to return to his See of Alexandria. Eusebius, who in the meantime had usurped the See of Constantinople, assembled a synod at Antioch and deposed St Athanasius, replacing him with an Arian, Gregory of Cappadocia. This act was enforced with the use of soldiers and their spears.

St Athanasius responded by going with two monks to Rome to lay his case before the new and assertive Pope, Julius I. The Pope proposed a council in Rome, only to be rejected by the Arians; presumably as such a council would be free from imperial and Eusebian interference.

Nevertheless, Pope Julius proceeded with his plan and fifty bishops (many of whom were dispossessed and fugitive bishops from the East) unanimously acquitted St Athanasius of all charges and restored him to his see (AD 341). Writing to the Arians, Pope Julius condemned the way they had acted to exclude the authority of the Bishop of Rome in the matter of St Athanasius: "And above all, why was nothing written to us about the Church of the Alexandrians? Are you ignorant that the custom has been to write first to us, and then for a just decision to be passed from this place?" Another Council headed by Ossius of Cordoba at Sardica (Sofia) attended by one hundred and seventy bishops (seventy-six from the East) reiterated Rome's decision two years later, reaffirming as well the Nicene Creed after the Arian faction stormed out. Feeling the pressure of the Catholic West and concerned about Egypt, Constantius II eventually permitted St Athanasius to return to his see in AD 346, where he would enjoy peace for the next ten years.

Eusebius died in AD 341, leaving behind as his legacy a lamentable state of division and conflict between East and West. The Arians now relied upon Constantius II as their most powerful champion. After the death of his brother Constantine II in AD 340 and the assassination of Constans in the Pyrennes AD 350 by the usurper Magnentius, Constantius II became sole Emperor, and with that Arianism began to penetrate deeply into the West. Constantius II achieved a marked success in AD 353 when he caused a Council at Arles to condemn Athanasius, where even the Papal Legates were induced to sign. This was followed by another Council at Milan in AD 355 which, dominated completely by Constantius II, condemned St Athanasius and exiled the following bishops: Pope Liberius (Julius I had died in AD 352), Ossius of Cordoba, St Hilary of Poitiers, Eusebius of Vercelli, Lucifer of Cagliari and Dionysius of Milan. The anti-Pope Felix II was set up in the place of Liberius, where he remained until AD 365. St Hilary would remain undaunted. While in exile in Phrygia, he continued to preach against Arianism and compiled his great treatise *On the Trinity* in twelve volumes. St Athanasius managed to escape soldiers sent to arrest him, and for some years hid in a monastery along the Nile and then in a desert grotto. Remarkably, from these hiding places he continued to govern his diocese and composed his great works against the Arians.

Emboldened by his success, Constantius II envisaged finally

burying the faith of Nicaea by composing a new compromised semi-Arian creed to be subscribed to by all.[1] To this creed he gained the signatures of Pope Liberius and Bishop Ossius through the infliction of suffering and threats of death.[2] After signing, both were permitted to return to their Sees (both afterwards never abjured the Nicene faith). The Emperor then envisaged calling a General Council to meet at Nicomedia in AD 360. His plan was temporarily thwarted by an earthquake that destroyed the cathedral and part of the city. Consequently, the Arians engineered two separate councils, one meeting in the West at Rimini and another in the East at Seleucia. At Seleucia the bishops signed an Arian formula called the Symbol of Nike without much debate; but in Rimini three hundred and twenty out of the four hundred bishops initially declared their adherence to the Nicene Creed, only to be forced by threats of exile and imprisonment to sign a vague semi-Arian formula. As for the rest of the bishops in the Empire, only a handful refused to sign it, including Pope Liberius. Of this time St Jerome would write: "The world groaned and was astonished to find itself Arian."

Themes for study:
- The intrigues, conspiracies and manipulations of Eusebius of Nicomedia.
- The support of the Emperor Constantius II for the cause of Arianism.
- The multiple councils called by the Nicene and Arian factions.
- The unbending resolve of the great St Athanasius against Arianism and its supporters.

---

[1] By this time the Arians had split into three factions: the *Semi-Arians*, who held that Christ was of like substance to the Father (*homoi-ousios*); the *Extreme Arians*, who held that Christ was utterly unlike the Father (*an-homoios*); and the *Middle Arians*, who, for the sake of reconciliation, simply affirmed that the Son was like the Father without referring to substance (*homoios*).

[2] The so-called "fall of Liberius" has historically been a controversial point. Though Sts Athanasius and Hilary clearly assert that he did 'fall', the 'Third Formula' signed by Pope Liberius was vague enough for him to append a declaration interpreting it in an orthodox sense.

Further reading:
- Warren H. Carroll, *The Founding of Christendom* (A History of Christendom), Vol. 2, Christendom Press, 1987, pp. 21-33.
- Fernard Hayward, *A History of the Popes*, J.M. Dent & Sons Ltd., 1931, pp. 45-51.
- Philip Hughes, *A History of the Church*, Vol. 1, Sheed and Ward, 1948, pp. 193-213.
- Fr John Laux, *Church History*, TAN Books and Publishers, 1930, pp. 113-118.

The Triumph of Orthodoxy

Arianism's apparent triumph would be short-lived. The Catholic counter-attack began with Pope Liberius issuing a public letter condemning the Council of Rimini. St Hilary of Poitiers returned to France and convoked the Council of Paris proclaiming the Nicene Creed in AD 362. St Athanasius and Lucifer of Cagliari from their places of exile accelerated the publication of tracts defending the Homo-ousion. St Cyril of Jerusalem, after possessing Semi-Arian sympathies, finally declared himself clearly on the Catholic side. Most significantly, Constantius II died on the 3 November AD 361, stripping Arianism of its most potent political supporter.

Constantius II was succeeded by Julian the Apostate. As his name suggests, Julian was no friend of Christianity at all, and sought to supplant its official favored status with a renewed syncretistic form of paganism. To further his plan, Julian allowed the exiled Catholic bishops to return to their dioceses with the sinister intention of igniting further confusion and conflict within the Church. However, the plan backfired, with St Athanasius reconciling many Semi-Arians who were disgusted with the actions of the hard-line Arians and feared the reappearance of a pagan on the throne. Julian was forced to act, exiling St Athanasius from Alexandria. This fourth exile would prove short-lived, for as St Athanasius had prophesied, Julian was a "little cloud" that would soon pass. While on campaign against Persia in AD 363, Julian received a spear in his side. Seeing the gush of blood, Julian uttered as his last words, "Thou hast triumphed, O Galilean."

Julian was succeeded by the Catholic, Jovian, who unfortunately died prematurely while taking instruction from St Athanasius in Antioch. The Empire was then divided into two again, the West going to the Catholic Valentinian; while the East was handed to the hard-line Arian Valens. For the next fourteen years, Valens strove to buttress the Arian cause, persecuting Catholics and even Semi-Arians, and forcing St Athanasius into his fifth exile in AD 367. This exile, again, proved to be brief, with the people of Alexandria compelling Valens to rescind his order through threats of violence after just four months. St Athanasius would again be among his people, remaining steadfast in orthodoxy and undisturbed until his death on 3 May AD 373.

There were other great men instrumental in the final triumph of the faith of Nicaea against Arianism and its offshoots. Most notable were the "Three Cappadocians": St Basil the Great, his dear friend St Gregory Nazianzus and St Basil's brother, St Gregory of Nyssa.

Born in Caesarea in Cappadocia around AD 330, St Basil was the eldest of ten children in a saintly family. His father was the son of St Macrina the Elder and his mother the daughter of a martyr. Besides himself, two of St Basil's brothers also became bishops and one of his sisters a model of the ascetical life. St Basil received his early education from his grandmother, who had learned it from the great St Gregory Thaumaturgus. Later, his father taught him rhetoric before going on to study in the schools of Caesarea, Constantinople and Athens. It was while in Athens that he formed his lasting friendship with St Gregory Nazianzus. Returning to Caesarea in AD 357, St Basil opened a school in rhetoric attracting students from across Asia Minor. It was his sister St Macrina the Younger who opened his eyes to the light of the Gospel: "I awoke as from deep sleep ... and prayed that a hand should come and lead me, and teach me the lessons of piety." After receiving baptism, St Basil journeyed throughout Egypt, the Middle East and Mesopotamia in search of a life of ascetical perfection. He, however, returned home and established together with his friend St Gregory a community of monks on the banks of the Iris River devoted to prayer, study and manual labor. Soon, disciples were flocking in from all sides, and St Basil organized them under a two-fold rule of thirty-five and three hundred and thirteen articles.

In AD 360, St Basil was forced to leave his secluded retreat and traveled to Constantinople with his bishop Dianus. There, he became directly embroiled in the conflict against Arianism and its offshoots. It was during this time of conflict that his great gifts were noticed and appreciated, and St Basil was elevated to the see of Caesarea in AD 370. He excelled as a man of action and government. His episcopal activity was manifold: he reformed clergy; he founded hospitals and poor houses; he wrote marvelous theological tracts against the Arians; he opposed the plans of the Emperor Valens in favor of Arianism; he won over the opponents of Nicaea; he assisted in bringing peace to the Church in Antioch; and he lobbied for aid from orthodox Catholics in the West.

Immediately after St Basil's death on 1 January AD 379, he was hailed as 'the Great' The Church has had few other men so richly gifted and talented. It was primarily through his strength of character, courage and prudence that St Basil held onto his see amidst the eastern deluge of Arianism. His intelligence, eloquence and character earned him the reputation of being "a Roman among the Greeks." The Council of Chalcedon (AD 451) would later call him the "greatest of the Fathers."

St Gregory Nazianzus was the second of the three great Cappadocians. He was born around the years AD 328-329 nearby the town of Nazianzus. His father, also named Gregory, had been a heretic (the sect of the Hypsistarii), but after his conversion effected through his pious wife was consecrated bishop of Nazianzus.

It was not until AD 360 that St Gregory was baptized. At the demand of his aging father's congregation, and to some extent against his will, St Gregory was ordained to the priesthood on Christmas AD 361. Excepting for a short stay at St Basil's monastery on the Iris River, St Gregory assisted his father in Nazianzus.

In AD 371, St Gregory was consecrated bishop of Sasima by St Basil who sought his assistance in his dispute against the Emperor Valens and the bishop of nearby Tyana. It was a miserable desert village crossroad in Cappadocia and St Gregory never took charge of it, remaining in Nazianzus assisting his father until his death in AD 374. St Gregory's abandonment of Sasima was the cause of an unhappy estrangement between him and St Basil.

St Gregory then withdrew to a retreat in Seleucia and, after hearing of St Basil's death in AD 379, was invited by the Nicene party to be their bishop in Constantinople, the long-time stronghold of the Arians. St Gregory accepted and in the small chapel of the *Anastasis* delivered his famous discourses on the Trinity to the beleaguered Catholic community and heretics who had come attracted by his sanctity, learning and eloquence. It was in Constantinople that he earned the title of *The Theologian* and "Defender of the Godhead of the Word."

During AD 378, Valens fell in battle against the Goths. The Catholic, Gratian, succeeded him. Gratian appointed another Catholic, Theodosius, to rule in the East. On 27 November AD 380, Theodosius installed St Gregory as the Archbishop of Constantinople. In this capacity he attended the First Council of Constantinople in May AD 381.

However, numerous objections were raised against his elevation to the Archbishopric on the grounds that it was uncanonical to transfer a bishop from one see to another. The opposition was so great that St Gregory resigned and returned to Nazianzus, where he took charge for two years before retiring to his family estate in solitude until his death around AD 389/390.

St Gregory of Nyssa was the younger brother of the great St Basil and the third of the Three Cappadocians. Born around AD 335, St Gregory was educated by his older brother and destined for the Church at a young age. However, after advancing to the office of lector, a crisis of conscience caused St Gregory to abandon a career in the Church for a worldly career as a teacher of rhetoric. This was despite the remonstrations of St Basil. He soon after also married a woman named Theosebeia. Their marriage did not last long due to Theosebeia's premature death. Due to the exhortations of his sister St Macrina and St Gregory Nazianzus, St Gregory of Nyssa returned to his true vocation and may have briefly stayed at St Basil's monastery on the Iris River for a retreat.

In AD 371, St Basil, intent on consolidating his own authority as metropolitan against the Arians, consecrated his younger brother as bishop of Nyssa, a small town between Caesarea and Ancyra. Like St Gregory of Nazianzus, this ordination was virtually against St Gregory of Nyssa's will, but unlike the former he did take possession of his diocese. It was as bishop of Nyssa that St Gregory's poor skills as an administrator came to the fore, much to the frustration of St Basil who strongly criticized and blamed his younger brother, calling him naïve and clumsy.

St Gregory of Nyssa was not gifted as a leader or preacher, but rather as a mystic, dogmatic theologian and writer. He was a philosopher who strove to harmonize the faith with reason and show their true accord. In his writings, we find nearly all species of Christian literature – the exegetical, dogmatico-polemical, ascetical, discourses and letters.

In AD 374, Valens had St Gregory of Nyssa deposed from his see. Further, in AD 376, the Arians falsely accused him of misappropriation of funds and persuaded the local governor of Pontus to order his arrest. St Gregory at first allowed himself to be arrested, but losing heart from the brutal treatment he received, escaped to a secret place of safety. St Gregory was then deposed as bishop in absentia by the Synod of Nyssa. For the next two years he wandered from town to town. He managed to regain his see in AD 378 after the death of the Emperor Valens, and was received with joy by the local populace.

After St Basil died in AD 379, a new era of activity began for St Gregory of Nyssa. He assisted at the Council of Antioch called in AD 379 to deal with the Meletian schism, and soon after visited Palestine. The Emperor Theodosius held St Gregory in high regard and his see was named in one of his edicts as a center of Catholic communion in the East. In AD 380, he was elected as Bishop of Sebaste in Armenia and attended the Council of Constantinople in AD 381 where he defended St Gregory Nazianzus and was looked upon as the heir to St Basil's thought.

After attending a synod at Constantinople in AD 394, St Gregory disappeared from the scene. He may have journeyed to Arabia at the behest of this synod to repress ecclesiastical disorders there and died soon afterwards.

Of final significance in the history of Arianism in the Roman Empire was the First Council of Constantinople, assembled by Theodosius in May AD 381. In the previous year, Theodosius had decreed that all in Constantinople "should live in the religion which the Apostle Peter had handed down to the Romans ...; 'hence that we believe in the one divinity of the Father and the Son and the Holy Spirit in equal majesty and holy Trinity'." Those who refused to subscribe to the Nicene Creed were ordered to surrender their churches. The Council was attended by 150 Catholic and 36 Semi-Arian/Macedonian bishops, however, none came from the West, nor was the Pope represented. All hard-line Arian bishops were excluded. The Council confirmed the Catholic succession to the See of Constantinople, reconciled the Semi-Arians, condemned Macedonianism and re-affirmed the Nicene Creed with an explicit confession of the divinity of the Holy Spirit as well.[1] With the closure of the Council of Constantinople, the Arian heresy was finally put to death officially. However, Arianism had been promoted beyond the Empire to the barbarian tribes north of the Danube, and would make a reappearance with their invasions of the fifth century.

---

[1] The Council of Constantinople later obtained the status of a full ecumenical council by virtue of the universal and enthusiastic acceptance of its confession of faith, especially by Popes Vigilius, Pelagius II and St Gregory the Great.

Themes for study:
- The Catholic counter-attack after Rimini and Seleucia.
- St Athanasius' steadfastness, exiles and final personal triumph.
- The lives and achievements of the "Three Cappadocians."
- The decrees of the Emperor Theodosius and the First Council of Constantinople.

Further reading:
- *The Catholic Encyclopaedia* (1911, vol. IV, p. 308).
- Warren H. Carroll, *The Founding of Christendom* (A History of Christendom), Vol. 2, Christendom Press, 1987, pp. 45-62.
- Philip Hughes, *A History of the Church*, Vol. 1, Sheed and Ward, 1948, pp. 214-230.
- Fr John Laux, *Church History*, TAN Books and Publishers, 1930, pp. 118-125.

AD 401 to AD 476: THE GREATEST OF THE FATHERS AND THE FALL OF ROME

The Genius of St Augustine of Hippo

Of all the Fathers of the Church, the greatest of all is St Augustine of Hippo. Jurgens at the beginning of his third volume makes the poignant comment, "If we were faced with the unlikely proposition of having to destroy completely either the works of Augustine or the works of all the other Fathers and Writers, I have little doubt that all the others would have to be sacrificed. Augustine will remain."[1] Dom Leclercq states, "He is also, perhaps, the one who most fully understood Christianity, who has felt it the most passionately; and in the twenty centuries of its history, we can see none but St Paul to whom he may be compared."

Aurelius Augustine was born in the small town of Tagaste in Numidia on 13 November AD 354, of a pagan father of loose morals and Christian mother. His father, Patricius, converted to Christianity in the fourteenth year of his marriage. His mother was the ever-famous model of motherhood, piety and perseverance, St Monica.

From the very beginning, St Monica instilled in Augustine a deep conviction of God's providence and a love of the name of Jesus: "The name of Thy Savior and Son had my tender heart, even with my mother's

---

[1] Rev. William A. Jurgens, *The Faith of the Early Fathers*, Copyright © 1970 by The Order of St Benedict, Inc., Vol. 3, p. 1.

milk, devoutly drunk in and deeply treasured." St Monica had her son signed with the cross and enrolled among the catechumens. Once, when very ill, St Augustine asked for baptism, but after the danger passed he unfortunately deferred receiving the sacrament according to the custom then in North Africa. During his early formal education in Tagaste and then Madaura, St Augustine clearly showed himself to be extraordinarily gifted.

Patricius, proud of his sons' intellectual achievements in the local schools, determined to send him to Carthage for advanced study. St Augustine was now seventeen years old. However, it was in Carthage that he fell into a dissolute lifestyle and entered an irregular relationship with a concubine; "banqueted upon iniquity", as he later described it. From this relationship was born his son, Adeodatus. The sixteen years that followed would be a long and thorny journey for St Augustine, a journey in which he had to wrestle against his pride, ambition, and sensuality.

At the age of nineteen, St Augustine began to develop a love for wisdom after reading Cicero's *Hortensius*. A crisis of faith as well as morals now began to devour him. In AD 374, he joined the sect of the Manichees, believing he had found in the teachings of Mani a wisdom higher than that taught by Christ. The attractions of this oriental sect were twofold: its deceptively simple teaching that evil was the creation of the god of Darkness, or the 'Evil Principle'; secondly, that not man himself, but the darkness within him, was the cause of personal sin. St Augustine went beyond being simply a Manichean by name but ardently attacked Christianity and strove to win as many converts as possible, including his closest friends. He officially became an 'auditor' among the Manichean hierarchy. In all, St Augustine would remain a Manichean for nine years.

During these wayward years, St Monica continued to pray for her son's conversion. At one point she became so disgusted with her son's anti-Christian opinions that she refused to even eat with him. However, she soon received him back again after a dream in which she was told that where she stood, there her son would one day be also. On one occasion while speaking to a bishop about how she feared for her son's salvation the bishop replied, "Go thy ways, and God bless thee, for it is impossible that the son of so many tears should perish."

Always searching for the truth, St Augustine eventually abandoned Manicheism in disgust when confronted with the ignorance of its supposed champion, Faustus of Milevis: the Manichees "destroyed, but built nothing." In AD 383, St Augustine secretly left Carthage for Rome to work as a lecturer in rhetoric, but he was unknown and the few students he had did not pay their fees. He therefore eagerly accepted a teaching position in oratory in Milan through the offices of the pagan Prefect of Rome, Symmachus. In Milan, St Augustine fell to the skepticism that was so fashionable among the pagans of the time, and soon despaired of ever knowing truth. The turning point came when some works of Plato and Plotinus came into his hands and he came to realize that God was the ultimate source of all being, truth and goodness and that evil was not a substance but rather a negation or defect. It was St Augustine's unwitting first step back to the Church.

It was while in Milan that he came into contact with St Ambrose and his preaching. He was introduced to the great bishop by a friend, who received St Augustine as a son: "I loved him not at first as a teacher of truth (which I had utterly despaired of in Thy Church), but as a person kind towards myself." It was St Ambrose who provided St Augustine with the ideal model of personal holiness and religious authority to move his will and pass from a study of Plato to the Epistles of St Paul. But the internal struggle within St Augustine was still raging, delaying his conversion: "Two wills, one old, one new; one of the flesh, one of the spirit, fought angrily together, and my soul was on the rack." His mother then arrived in Milan and arranged for him a marriage that fell through due to the bride's tender age. St Augustine finally dismissed his concubine after fifteen years, only to take up another.

The decision to convert came in August AD 386. St Augustine heard of the sudden conversion of two Roman military officers who abandoned their careers and embraced the monastic life: "The unlearned start up and take heaven by violence, while we with all our learning ... wallow in flesh and blood." Then St Augustine heard the voice of a child singing a song with the refrain, *"Tolle lege, tolle lege"* ("Pick up and read, pick up and read"). He opened at random a volume of St Paul's letters and read the following: "not in debauchery and licentiousness, not in quarreling and jealousy. But put on the Lord Jesus Christ, and make no provision for the flesh, to gratify its desires" (Rom. 13:13-14). In April AD 387, in the presence of his mother, St Augustine, his son Adeodatus and his best friend Alypius received baptism at the hands of St Ambrose:

"Thou hast made us for Thyself, O God, and our hearts are restless until they find their rest in Thee." Only a few months later, St Monica was to die after sharing the famous ecstasy of Ostia with her now converted son. St Augustine's description of his mother's saintly death and his grief make some of the most exquisite reading in all literature.

One must never underestimate the role of St Monica. For sixteen years she persevered in prayer for her son's conversion and the regulation of his relationship. But even she had no idea that her perseverance would bring forth not only a conversion, but also a bishop, a confessor and defender of the Faith, a Father and Doctor of the Church and foremost above all, a Saint. St Augustine would write later that, "She leaped for joy, and triumphed, and blessed Thee, Who art able to do above that which we ask or think ..."

After his mother's death, St Augustine returned to Africa. Three years of monastic life in Tagaste (during which Adeodatus died) was followed by his reluctant ordination to the priesthood in AD 391 by Bishop Valerius. In AD 395, St Augustine was consecrated co-bishop of Hippo by the same bishop. A year later he was bishop of Hippo in his own right. Despite his episcopal ordination, St Augustine continued to live a monastic lifestyle among a religious and clerical community in his residence, all supported from a common fund. From this community, ten of St Augustine's contemporary associates would be promoted to the episcopacy.

As bishop, besides the daily duties of administering his diocese, directing his clergy, and instructing and sanctifying his people, St Augustine used his pen to author the largest surviving Patristic corpus of letters and sermons (approximately four hundred). His *Confessions* and *The City of God Against the Pagans* will always remain two of the greatest literary treasures of Christianity. His *De Trinitate* is the most important of his dogmatic works. He also authored a Rule for religious life and combated all the major heresies of his day, in particular Manicheism, Arianism, Donatism and Pelagianism. He also dealt with exegesis, mathematics, aesthetics, music, grammar and poetry.

Donatism had existed for nearly a century when St Augustine was ordained bishop. At first he tried to win the Donatists over through discussions and interviews. But the Donatists broke off all discussion and escalated violence and assassination attempts on Catholic bishops, including St Augustine himself. As a consequence, he called upon the aid of the Emperor Honorius to suppress them. In AD 411, the Emperor ordered a conference of Catholic and Donatist bishops at Carthage. The imperial delegate, Marcellinus gave victory on all points to the Catholics, and for his trouble was later murdered by the disgruntled Donatists. After the Catholic victory, conversions increased and repression continued. The last remnants of Donatism were wiped out with the Saracen invasion in the late seventh century.

Founded by an Irish monk named Pelagius (+AD 418), Pelagianism denied the supernatural elevation of humanity by asserting that Adam and Eve were created only in a natural state without sanctifying grace. Consequently, the Fall had no effect on them and their children by way of loss of grace; the only effect of original sin on others was by way of setting bad example. Hence, sin is not contracted through natural generation but is learnt from the scandal of others. It follows, further, that the children of Adam are born naturally good and are in no need of a Redeemer. Christ's act of redemption is thus reduced to providing lofty teaching and virtuous example, while forgiveness of sin through faith means forgiveness from punishment, not renewal in grace. If the children of Adam keep good company and direct their wills and ordinary powers to live a sinless and holy life, they can achieve eternal beatitude through their own natural efforts.

Though meeting sporadic opposition in Rome, Carthage and in the East, it was St Augustine who rose to combat Pelagianism with his powerful pen: "They (the Pelagians) contend that in this life there are or have been righteous men having no sin at all. By this presumption they most clearly contradict the Lord's Prayer, in which all the members of Christ cry aloud with true heart these words to be said each day: 'Forgive us our debts.'"[2] For the self-confident Pelagian, the Lord's Prayer served only as a profession of humility, not a statement of fact.

St Augustine drew on the parable of the vine and the branches (John 15:1) to strike at Pelagianism and expose it as a novelty contrary to the teachings of Christ. Only when the vital union between Christ (the vine) and His members (the branches) is established is it possible to bring forth supernatural fruit: for "apart from me you can do nothing" (John

---

[2] *Against Two Letters of the Pelagians* 4, 10, 27 (AD 420).

15:5). St Augustine also presented this particular thought: "Could we bring together here in living form all the saints of both sexes and question them whether they were without sin, would they not exclaim unanimously: 'If we say that we have no sin, we deceive ourselves, and the truth is not in us'?"[3] Before the entire world St Augustine attested that, "Such is the Pelagian heresy, not ancient, but having sprung up a short time ago."[4]

St Augustine's fifteen treatises against Pelagianism would earn him the title of 'Doctor of Grace.' In AD 416, the Councils of Carthage and Milevis condemned and excommunicated Pelagius for his teachings. Pope Innocent I confirmed the decisions, causing St Augustine to joyfully exclaim, "Rome has spoken, the matter is now at an end." Pope Zosimus the following year reaffirmed the condemnation and Pelagius was expelled from the western Empire, finding refuge in Constantinople.

Arguably, St Augustine's most important work was *The City of God*, begun in AD 413 in response to pagan attacks that the sacking of Rome in AD 410 by the Visigoths was due to the abandonment of the old pagan gods. For successive centuries the old gods had preserved Rome; just one century of Christianity sufficed to bring ruin upon the Eternal City. St Augustine argued instead that all the virtues found in the Greeks, Romans and Hebrews were fulfilled in, and exceeded by Christ. He expressed as well a philosophy of history, noting that only Christianity could tie together and relate the whole of human history from the beginning of time to the end of the world. It is the divine light that illumines the story of humanity. For St Augustine, the "City of God" is founded upon love of God and contempt of self; in contrast, the "City of Man" is founded upon love of self. These cities exist side by side, moving each to its own destiny.

In AD 426, St Augustine went into semi-retirement handing over most of his episcopal duties to concentrate on his writings. The invasion of the Vandals marked the end of his prolific life and works. St Augustine died in Hippo on 28 August AD 430, while the barbarians laid siege to the city. His influence will remain for as long as the Church itself.

---

[3] *On Nature and Grace* 36 (AD 415).
[4] *Grace and Free Choice* 6 (AD 426).

Themes for study:
- St Augustine's early years and his fall into moral degeneracy.
- St Augustine's Manichean period.
- The prayers of his mother, St Monica, and St Augustine's dramatic conversion.
- St Augustine's life as a bishop, a confessor and defender of the Faith, a Father and Doctor of the Church.

Further reading:
- *The Catholic Encyclopaedia* (1911, vol. II, pp. 84-103).
- Anne W. Carroll, *Christ the King: Lord of History*, Second Edition, Trinity Communications, 1986, pp. 109-110.
- Philip Hughes, *A History of the Church*, Vol. 1, Sheed and Ward, 1948, pp. 142-143.
- Fr John Laux, *Church History*, TAN Books and Publishers, 1930, pp. 138-151.

The Nestorian and Monophysite Heresies

Nestorius was originally a monk from Antioch, of austere life and great eloquence. In AD 428, he was elevated to the position of Patriarch of Constantinople. On Christmas day AD 428, Nestorius delivered a sermon from the pulpit of his Cathedral containing the following words: "Mary did not bear God. The creature did not bear the Creator, but the man ... He who was formed in the womb of Mary was not God Himself, but God assumed him." Though immediately challenged from within the congregation, Nestorius continued to develop his theme in a series of sermons, saying, "How could she be the mother of Him who is of a different nature than herself?" Clergy and monks who opposed Nestorius found themselves excommunicated and deposed, some were even scourged and imprisoned.

Nestorius' underlying problem was his denial of Christ as *one divine Person* with two natures, human and divine, asserting rather that Christ was *two Persons, one human and one divine*, with two natures, human and divine. Further, these two persons were not united but separate, thus rejecting the hypostatic union. Instead, the divine only dwelt in Christ as in a temple. Consequently, the Virgin Mary, as she supplied only Christ's human flesh and not His divinity, was only mother of Christ the man. She could be called *Christotokos* (mother of Christ), but in no sense could she be called *Theotokos* (Mother of God).

Copies of Nestorius' sermons containing his novel teaching soon spread rapidly. St Cyril, bishop of Alexandria, on hearing of it himself asked the question, "Is her son God, or is he not?" St Cyril refuted Nestorius, demanded a retraction, and appealed to Pope Celestine when none was forthcoming: "The ancient custom of the Church admonishes us that matters of this kind should be communicated to Your Holiness." Nestorius, too, sent his views to Pope Celestine. On 11 August AD 430, Celestine pronounced Nestorius to be heretical and gave him ten days to renounce his views or face deposition. Nestorius paid no attention to the Pope's ultimatum and declared his doctrine to be correct; furthermore, his condemnation was the work of the Church of Alexandria, which was jealous of Constantinople. Nestorius received open support from John of Antioch and most of the bishops of Syria.

Nestorius' obstinacy raised the controversy to boiling point. In response, the eastern Emperor, Theodosius II, called for an ecumenical council, which was approved by Pope Celestine. The council was summoned to meet in Ephesus on 22 June AD 431, and was to assemble in the Church of the Theotokos, near the place where the Virgin Mary actually lived with St John. St Cyril presided over the Council of Ephesus as vicegerent of the Pope ("filling the place of the most holy and blessed Archbishop of the Roman Church, Celestine"), which in its first session attended by about one hundred and sixty bishops (by the end of the day there were one hundred and ninety-eight), condemned, deposed and excommunicated Nestorius. Mary was indeed the Mother of God, as Jesus Christ was one divine Person with two natures, human and divine. A mother is a mother of a person, not simply of a nature. Being mother of a divine person, Mary was entitled to be called Theotokos, or God-bearer.

The entire proceedings of the first session were concluded in the one day. It was night when St Cyril opened the doors of the church to announce the Council's decision to the waiting crowd. Hearing the words *"Maria Theotokos"* from St Cyril's lips, the crowd erupted with joyful shouts of *"Theotokos!, Theotokos!"* The people of Ephesus then formed torchlight processions and escorted the bishops in triumph to their lodgings. For the remainder of the night the city was brightly illuminated. A notification addressed to "the new Judas" was sent by the Council to Nestorius; he refused to receive it so it was attached to his door.

Arriving with thirty-four bishops five days after the close of the first session, John of Antioch called together those bishops friendly to Nestorius and declared the actions taken against him null and void, and excommunicated St Cyril and the bishop of Ephesus, Memnon. Further sessions on 10, 16, 31 July and 11 September re-affirmed the decision of 22 June, especially after one of the Papal Legates, the priest Philip, declared it to be valid and good in law: "This is a just judgment. To Celestine the new Paul!" Theodosius considered deposing St Cyril, Nestorius and Memnon together in order to bring peace, but was prevailed upon by his sister Pulcheria to ratify the Council and banish only Nestorius to Antioch. Later, Nestorius was banished again to Egypt for continuing to spread his errors. Pope Celestine's successor, St Sixtus III, confirmed the Council's decrees.

Some argue that Nestorius was condemned before he even arrived in Ephesus. Nevertheless, when called upon three times to defend his teachings he refused on each occasion to appear. Defending the decrees of the Council of Ephesus even in the face of imperial opposition and imprisonment became thereafter St Cyril's life work. John of Antioch and his supporters were reconciled in AD 433, while Nestorius died miserable and impenitent in his place of exile in the deserts of Upper Egypt around AD 450. His heresy never gained a very large following, but survived in Iraq and Persia and from there spread as far east as India, China and Java.

In reaction to Nestorianism another heresy arose, that of Monophysitism. Eutyches of Constantinople, in his zeal to oppose Nestorius and assert the unity of Christ's Person, taught that Christ had only one nature (*monophysis*), the Divine nature, and that his human nature was completely subsumed in it like a drop of water in wine. This teaching gained acceptance from many in Alexandria, who in support of their position quoted the now deceased St Cyril of Alexandria (hence their designation as "the Cyrillians" in this dispute).

Flavian, Patriarch of Constantinople, acted quickly to root out this heresy by deposing and excommunicating Eutyches. However, Eutyches remained obstinate, and was confirmed in his position by Dioscorus, Patriarch of Alexandria. Dioscorus convinced the Emperor Theodosius II to convene a general council, with him as head, to be held in Ephesus and set down for 8 August AD 449. Dioscorus was intent on manipulating the council proceedings in his favor and so refused to recognize Pope Leo the Great's representatives, Julius and Hilary, alleging bias for having dined recently with Flavian. The Papal Legates had with them a document prepared by Pope Leo (and later known as the *Tome of Leo*) declaring that Christ was one divine Person possessing two complete and perfect natures, divine and human. When a statement to this effect was read out to the one hundred and thirty council Fathers, Dioscorus led the Monophysite party to shout it down. He then declared Monophysitism approved by the council, acquitted and reinstated Eutyches, and deposed Flavian and his supporters. A riot ensued in which Hilary and Flavian were beaten, Flavian dying of his injuries during his return to Constantinople. Hilary managed to escape and made his way back to Rome, reporting what had happened during the council. Pope Leo condemned the council as *latrodinium*, and so it entered into history as the "Robber Council of Ephesus."

Pope Leo responded further by excommunicating Dioscorus and calling for another and greater general council. This demand was ignored by Theodosius II, but was granted by his immediate successor, Marcian. So, on 8 October AD 451, the Council of Chalcedon was convened with nearly six hundred bishops in attendance. The actions of Dioscorus were discussed and reprobated, together with the declarations of the Robber Council. The Tome of Leo was finally presented to the bishops and received enthusiastically: "That is the faith of the Fathers; that is the faith of the Apostles! So we all believe! Peter has spoken through Leo!"

However, as with the Arian heresy, the decision of an ecumenical council failed to end the troubles. The non-Greek speaking churches of Egypt, Syria, Ethiopia and Armenia severed themselves from the rest of the Church, proudly asserting themselves as "non-Chalcedonian." Throughout the next one hundred years, the Monophysites would agitate against Chalcedon, seeking the support of those in political power to impose their doctrine. Their most powerful political ally was the wife of the Byzantine Emperor Justinian (AD 527-565), namely Theodora.

Justinian was a Catholic but was obsessed with dreams of re-establishing the old Roman Empire, and so allowed Theodora to take care of religious affairs. Theodora had adopted Monophysitism from Egyptian monks who fed her while she was only an unemployed circus dancer. In her now powerful position of Empress, she wanted to install Monophysites into the great sees of Rome and Constantinople, namely Vigilius and Anthimius.

Vigilius had accepted seven hundred pounds of gold from Theodora and the promise of the Papacy if he cooperated with her heretical agenda. Anthimius was the first to be installed, but was immediately deposed by the holy Pope Agapetus who happened to be in Constantinople in February AD 536. Soon after, the Pope mysteriously died, most probably through the machinations of Theodora and Vigilius. In June AD 536, Agapetus was succeeded by Silverius. Theodora demanded of him the restoration of Anthimius. Upon being refused, Theodora ordered her general Belisarius to seize Pope Silverius and send him into exile. Vigilius then arranged for his painful death by starvation on the island of Palmyria off the coast of Naples.

Now that Silverius was dead, the Byzantine army in Rome pressured the clergy to recognize Vigilius as his legitimate successor. This they did, giving Theodora what finally seemed to be complete victory. However, as Pope, Vigilius underwent an extraordinary turnaround. The former ambitious, greedy and murderous heretic began to detach himself from Theodora and speak out forcibly in favor of orthodoxy: "Formerly I spoke wrongly and foolishly; now I assuredly refuse to restore a man who is a heretic. Though unworthy, I am Vicar of the Blessed Peter the Apostle, as were my predecessors, the holy Agapetus and Silverius."

Theodora was furious, and had Vigilius arrested and brought to Constantinople in January AD 547. There, he was imprisoned and endured constant pressure to submit. After Theodora died in AD 548, Justinian continued the pressure, leaving the Pope in confinement for a further seven years. An ecumenical council held in Constantinople in AD 553 once again anathematized Monophysitism, but also in the so-called "Three Chapters" condemned Theodore of Mopsuestia and Theodoret of Cyr for alleged Nestorianism, though they had both been acquitted at Chalcedon as free of this heresy. For his initial opposition to this latter action, Vigilius was exiled for six months to an island in the Sea of Marmara, but on being brought back to Constantinople, condemned the doctrines described in the "Three Chapters" and was thereupon allowed by Justinian to return to Rome. However, while in Sicily during the return journey, Vigilius died (7 January AD 555). Though Monophysitism continues to this day, it remains mostly confined to the Egyptian, Syrian, Armenian and Ethiopian Orthodox Churches of the Middle East.

Themes for study:
- Nestorius and the denial of the unity of Christ in one divine Person.
- The Council of Ephesus.
- Eutyches and the denial of Christ's true humanity.
- The Council of Chalcedon.

Further reading:
- Anne W. Carroll, *Christ the King: Lord of History*, Second Edition, Trinity Communications, 1986, pp. 112-116.
- Fernard Hayward, *A History of the Popes*, J.M. Dent & Sons Ltd., 1931, pp. 65-81.
- Philip Hughes, *A History of the Church*, Vol. 1, Sheed and Ward, 1948, pp. 236-290.
- Fr John Laux, *Church History*, TAN Books and Publishers, 1930, pp. 153-157.

The Barbarian Invasions up to AD 476

Pressure on the borders of the Empire from barbarian tribes gradually increased throughout the fourth century AD. During the reign of Valentinian I (AD 364-375), successive German raids across the Rhine and Danube Rivers were met and defeated. Part of Valentinian's success was due to his construction of a complex system of new defenses, and his deliberate stirring up of dissensions between rival tribes. In the meantime, numerous German barbarians continued to be admitted within the western frontiers. Valentinian was so successful in his defensive campaigns that by the time of his sudden death the western Empire appeared to be as strong as ever.

In AD 378, however, the eastern Empire was to suffer a shock of unprecedented gravity. Coming originally from central Asia, the Huns gradually moved westwards, and around the year AD 370 burst into the Ukrainian kingdom of the Goths. The Gothic state crumbled and two hundred thousand refugees crossed the Danube into the Balkans. The Roman authorities permitted the Goths to settle, but incensed at the unjust treatment handed out by their hosts, their chieftain, Fritigern, broke into revolt and led his people to ravage the countryside. The eastern Emperor Valens led an army from Asia Minor to deal with the crisis, and met the Goths at Adrianople in Thrace. The Gothic cavalry drove off the Roman horsemen, leaving the imperial infantry exposed and massacred almost to the last man. Valens himself fell, his corpse disappearing without trace.

Valens' successor, Theodosius I, in AD 382 allowed the Goths to settle within the boundaries of the Empire under their own rulers, on condition that they supply soldiers and agricultural workers for the Romans – the beginning of the so-called 'federate status' that would be given to various nations that penetrated into the Empire. It was hoped that the granting of such status would regulate the entry of barbarian tribes and allow for their eventual assimilation. But the whole design was overwhelmed by the events of 31 December AD 405. On that day a combined army of barbarians from different tribes – Vandals, Suevi, Alans, Burgundians – crossed the frozen Rhine River and, sweeping aside meager resistance, fanned out across the whole of Gaul, ravaging towns and the countryside. Only Toulouse of all the Gallic cities put up a fight. It was the decisive incursion; the Rhine defenses would never be secure again. In the meantime, Britain was denuded of troops, allowing the island to gradually pass into the hands of Saxon immigrants who had recently entered and settled from northern Germany.

Simultaneously, the Visigoths under their new leader, Alaric, moved from the Balkans into northern Italy, and began making demands on the Romans for gold and land. At first, the Roman Senate voted to grant him four thousand pounds of gold, but later refused other hefty demands. In two successive years he compelled the Romans to grant him his wishes by marching his army right up to the walls of Rome. On the third occasion in AD 410, the gates of the city were treacherously opened to him. For three days, the Visigoths plundered and burned throughout the ancient capital. It was the first sacking of Rome for nearly eight hundred years, and horrified the entire Empire. St Jerome, in faraway Bethlehem, thought that it was the end of the world. Soon after, Alaric died and the Visigoths were allowed to settle in southwestern France under federate status with Toulouse as their capital (AD 418).

The Vandals, likewise, refused to remain still and crossed Spain into North Africa in AD 429 under their new leader, Genseric. A joint western and eastern Empire army sent against them failed dismally, and the Romans, with the Rhine frontier still defenseless and peasant revolts breaking out throughout Gaul, felt compelled to offer a peace treaty, the terms of which granted the Vandals federate status in Morocco and western Algeria. But after ten years, Genseric cast aside this treaty and besieged and captured Carthage, the second most important city in the west. Furthermore, he threw off all pretense of federate status and ruled his North African dominions free from all Roman interference. Genseric was also unique in possessing his own fleet, severing the unity of the Mediterranean for the first time in six hundred years. The dissolution of the Empire was now a de facto reality.

To add to the Empire's woes, the Huns were also beginning to impact upon the ever more fragile Empire. By AD 434, under their new leader, Attila (otherwise known as the 'Scourge of God'), they ruled the vast territories between the Baltic Sea and the Danube. During the AD 440's, Attila concentrated his attacks on the eastern Empire, before turning against the West in the hope of added booty. In AD 451, Attila led his forces into Gaul, and on the Catalaunian Plains confronted a combined army of Romans and federated Germans, mostly Goths. The Romans achieved a great victory, which was Attila's first defeat. Attila retired his forces across the Alps with the plan of plundering Italy. Successful in the north, Attila then prepared to cross one of the Po tributaries, only to be confronted with the figure of Pope Leo the Great who had journeyed all the way north from Rome with priests, monks and deacons bearing crosses and banners. Pope Leo had no army, but made full use of his authority as the political potentate of the once great capital. Attila was convinced to turn away from Rome on the grounds that famine and pestilence then plaguing Italy would prevent his forces feeding off the countryside. Others say, that while speaking to Pope Leo, Attila saw behind him an apparition of St Peter with a flaming sword ready o strike any would-be attacker. In any case, the Huns turned back, and only two years later Attila was dead and the vast Hunnish kingdom rapidly broke up. By AD 455, the surviving Huns were back in the distant east, never to be a powerful force again.

Nevertheless, Rome would be visited with catastrophe in the fateful year of AD 455. Genseric with his Vandals landed in person at Ostia, and then launched an assault against the Eternal City. There was no Emperor or army to stop them. For two whole weeks the defenseless city was plundered by looting far beyond that inflicted by Alaric nearly fifty years earlier. Pope Leo I again intervened, preventing wholesale murder and burning and the sacking of the largest churches. On his departure, Genseric took thousands of captives as slaves, leaving a shattered and empty shell of a city.

The twenty-one years that followed saw nine more or less legitimate rulers of the western Empire come and go, six of them coming to violent ends. These rulers governed from Ravenna, the last being Romulus Augustulus. Given the throne by his father at the age of only fourteen, Romulus remained Emperor for less than a year. The general Odoacer, who commanded an army of Danubian compatriots within Italy, began demanding federate status within that peninsula. Upon being rejected, Odoacer's troops declared him as their independent king and marched on Ravenna. Romulus was deposed and pensioned off into exile in Dalmatia. The eastern Emperor, Zeno, continued to recognize Romulus as the legitimate ruler, nevertheless, took no immediate action against Odoacer. Independent barbarian kings now ruled what was once the western Empire: Visigoths in Spain; Vandals in North Africa; Franks in Gaul; Ostrogoths and Lombards in Italy; Angles, Saxons and Jutes in Britain. There would never be another Emperor of a united West. It was the year AD 476. The Western Roman Empire had finally fallen.

However, the Church survived, to continue building that new civilization, the cornerstone of which had already been laid nearly four hundred and fifty years earlier.

Themes for study:
- The Gothic victory at Adrianople in AD 378.
- The crossing of the Rhine by a combined barbarian force on 31 December AD 405.
- The sackings of Rome in AD 410 and 455.
- The final fall of the Western Empire in AD 476.

Further reading:
- Anne W. Carroll, *Christ the King: Lord of History*, Second Edition, Trinity Communications, 1986, pp. 118-120.
- *The Catholic Encyclopaedia* (1911, vol. XV, pp. 268-269).
- Michael Grant, *History of Rome*, Book Club Associates, 1978, pp. 321-331.
- Fr John Laux, *Church History*, TAN Books and Publishers, 1930, pp. 173-176.

Appendices

Appendix A - Popes of the Early Church AD 30-476

St Peter (+C. 67)
St Linus (67 - 76)
St Anacletus (76 - 88)
St Clement (88 - 97)
St Evaristus (97 - 105)
St Alexander I (105 - 115)
St Sixtus I (115 - 125)
St Telesphorus (125 - 136)
St Hyginus (136 - 140)
St Pius I (140 - 155)
St Anicetus (155 - 166)
St Soter (166 - 175)
St Eleutherius (175 - 189)
St Victor I (189 - 199)
St Zephyrinus (199 - 217)
St Callistus (217 - 222)
St Urban I (222 - 230)
St Pontian (230 - 235)
St Anterus (235 - 236)
St Fabian (236 - 250)
St Cornelius (251 - 253)
St Lucius I (253 - 254)
St Stephen I (254 - 257)
St Sixtus II (257 - 258)

St Dionysius (259 - 268)
St Felix I (269 - 274)
St Eutychian (275 - 283)
St Caius (283 - 296)
St Marcellinus (296 - 304)
St Marcellus I (308 - 309)
St Eusebius
   (April 309 - Aug. 309)
St Melchiades (311 - 314)
St Sylvester I (314 - 335)
St Marcus (Jan. 336 - Oct. 336)
St Julius I (337 - 352)
Liberius (352 - 366)
St Damasus I (366 - 384)
St Siricius (384 - 399)
St Anastasius I (399 - 401)
St Innocent I (401 - 417)
St Zozimus (417 - 418)
St Boniface I (418 - 422)
St Celestine (422 - 432)
St Sixtus III (432 - 440)
St Leo I the Great (440 - 461)
St Hilary (461 - 468)
St Simplicius (468 - 483)

Appendix B - Roman Emperors from the time of Christ to AD 476[1]

	Eastern Empire	Western Empire
Augustus (27 BC)		
Tiberius (14 AD)		
Caligula (37)	Diocletian (284)	Maximin 284
Claudius (41)	Galerius (305)	Constantius I (305)
Neros (54)		Constantine I (306)
Galba (68)	Licinius (311)	
Otho (68)	Constantine I (324)	
Vitellius (69)	Constantius II (337)	Constans I (337)
Vespasian (69)		Constantius II (351)
Titus (79)	Julian (361)	Julian (361)
Domitian (81)	Jovian (363)	Jovian (363)
Nerva (96)	Valens (364)	Valentinian I (364)
Trajan (98)	Theodosius I (379)	Gratian (375)
Hadrian (117)		Valentinian II (382)
Antoninus Pius (138)		Theodosius I (392)
Marcus Aurelius (161)	Arcadius (395)	Honorius (395)
Commodus (180)	Theodosius II (408)	
Septimus Severus (193)		Valentinian III (425)[2]
Caracalla (211)	Marcian (450)	
Heliogabalus (218)	Leo I (457)	
Alexander Severus (222)	Zeno (474)	
Maximin Thrax (235)		Romulus Augustulus (476)
The Gordians (238)		
Philip the Arab (244)		
Decius (249)		
Gallus (251)		
Valerian (253)		
Gallienus (260)		
Claudius II (268)		
Aurelian (270)		
Tacitus (275)		
Probus (276)		
Carus (282)		

---

[1] The single date against the Emperor's name is the date of his accession.
[2] The last effective Emperor in the West.

Appendices

Appendix C - Creeds of the Early Church
1ˢᵗ -5ᵗʰ Centuries AD

THE APOSTLES' CREED
(DATE UNKNOWN)

I believe in God, the Father Almighty, Creator of heaven and earth; and in Jesus Christ, His only Son, Our Lord; Who was conceived by the Holy Spirit, born of the Virgin Mary, suffered under Pontius Pilate, was crucified, died, and was buried. He descended into hell; the third day He rose again from the dead; He ascended into heaven, sitteth at the right hand of God, the Father Almighty; from thence He shall come to judge the living and the dead. I believe in the Holy Spirit, the Holy Catholic Church, the communion of saints, the forgiveness of sins, the resurrection of the body, and life everlasting. Amen.

THE DER-BALIZEH PAPYRUS
(c. LATE 2ⁿᵈ CENTURY AD)

I believe in God, the Father almighty, and in His only-begotten Son, Jesus Christ, and in the Holy Spirit, and in the resurrection of the flesh, and in the Holy Catholic Church.

THE CREED OF ST IRENAEUS OF LYONS
(*Against Heresies* 1, 10, 1)
(c. AD 180)

For the Church, although dispersed throughout the whole world even to the ends of the earth, has received from the Apostles and from their disciples the faith in one God, Father Almighty, the Creator of heaven and earth and sea and all that is in them; and in one Jesus Christ, the Son of God who became flesh for our salvation; and in the Holy Spirit, who announced through the prophets the dispensations and the comings, and the birth from a Virgin, and the passion, and the resurrection from the dead, and the bodily ascension into heaven in the glory of the Father to re-establish all things; and the raising up again of all flesh of all humanity, in order that to Jesus Christ our Lord and God and Savior and King, in accord with the approval of the invisible Father, every knee shall bend of those in heaven and on earth and under the earth, and that every tongue shall confess Him, and that He may make just judgment of them all; and that He may send the spiritual forces of wickedness and the angels who transgressed and became apostates, and the impious, unjust, lawless and blasphemous amongst men, into everlasting fire; and that He may grant life, immortality, and surround with eternal glory the just and the holy, and those who have kept His commands and who have persevered in His love, either from the beginning or from their repentance.

THE CREED OF TERTULLIAN
(*Against Praxeas* 2, 1)
(Post AD 213)

We do indeed believe that there is only one God; but we believe that under this dispensation ... there is also a Son of this one only God, His Word, who proceeded from Him and through whom all things were made and without whom nothing was made. We believe that He was sent by the Father into a Virgin and was born of her, God and man, Son of man and Son of God, and was called by the name Jesus Christ. We believe that He suffered and that, in accord with the Scriptures, He died and was buried; and that He was raised again by the Father to resume His place in heaven, sitting at the right of the Father; and that He will come to judge the living and the dead. We believe that He sent down from the Father, in accord with His own promise, the Holy Spirit, the Paraclete, the Sanctifier of the faith of those who believe in the Father and in the Son and in the Holy Spirit...That this rule of faith has been current since the beginning of the Gospel, before even the earlier heretics, — much more then, before Praxeas, who was but of yesterday...

THE APOSTOLIC TRADITION OF ST HIPPOLYTUS
(c. AD 215-217)

Do you believe in God, the Father almighty?

Do you believe in Jesus Christ, the Son of God, who was born of the Virgin Mary by the Holy Spirit, has been crucified under Pontius Pilate, died [and was buried], who, on the third day
rose again, alive, from the dead, ascended into heaven and took His seat at the right hand of the Father, and shall come to judge the living and the dead?
Do you believe in the Holy Church and the resurrection of the body in the Holy Spirit?

THE SYMBOL OF EUSEBIUS
(AD 325)

We believe in one God, the Father almighty, the maker of all things visible and invisible. And in one Lord Jesus Christ, the Word of God, God from God, light from light, Life from Life, the only-begotten Son, first born of all creation, begotten from the Father before all ages, through whom all things were made. For our salvation He became flesh and lived as a man, He suffered and rose again on the third day and ascended to the Father. He shall come again in glory to judge the living and the dead. We believe also in one Holy Spirit.

SYMBOL OF THE FIRST GENERAL COUNCIL OF NICAEA
(AD 325)

We believe in one God, the Father almighty, maker of all things, visible and invisible. And in one Lord Jesus Christ, the Son of God, the only-begotten generated from the Father, that is, from the being of the Father, God from God, Light from Light, true God from true God, begotten, not made, one in being with the Father, through whom all things were made, those in heaven and those on earth. For us men and for our salvation He came down, and became flesh, was made man, suffered, and rose again on the third day. He ascended to the heavens and shall come again to judge the living and the dead. And in the Holy Spirit.

As for those who say: "There was a time when He was not" and "Before being begotten He was not", and who declare that He was made from nothing, or that the Son of God is from a different substance or being, that is, created or subject to change and alteration, such persons the Catholic Church condemns.

THE SYMBOL OF ST CYRIL OF JERUSALEM
(c. AD 348)

We believe in one God, the Father almighty, maker of heaven and earth, of all things visible and invisible. And in one Lord Jesus Christ, the only-begotten Son of God, generated from the Father, true God before all the ages, through whom all things were made. He [came down, became flesh and] was made man, was crucified [and buried]. He rose again [from the dead] on the third day, and ascended to the heavens, and took His seat at the right hand of the Father. He shall come in glory to judge the living and the dead; to His Kingdom there will be no end. And in one Holy Spirit, the Paraclete, who has spoken in the prophets, and in one baptism of conversion for the forgiveness of sins, and in one Holy and Catholic Church, and in the resurrection of the body, and the life everlasting.

THE SYMBOL OF ST EPIPHANIUS OF SALAMIS
(AD 374)

We believe in one God, the Father almighty, maker of heaven and earth, of all things visible and invisible. And in one Lord Jesus Christ, the only-begotten Son of God, generated from the Father before all ages, that is, from the being of the Father, Light from Light, true God from true God, begotten, not made, one in being with the Father, through whom all things were made, those in the heavens and those on earth. For us men and for our salvation He came down from the heavens, and became flesh from the Holy Spirit and the Virgin Mary, and was made man. For our sake too He was crucified under Pontius Pilate, suffered and was buried. On the third day He rose again according to the Scriptures. He ascended to the heavens and is seated at the right hand of the Father. He shall come again in glory to judge the living and the dead; to His Kingdom there will be no end. And in the Holy Spirit, the Lord and Giver of life, who proceeds from the Father, who together with the Father and the Son is worshipped and glorified, who has spoken through the prophets. (And) in one Holy, Catholic and apostolic Church. We acknowledge one baptism for the forgiveness of sins. We expect the resurrection of the dead and the life of the world to come. Amen.

As for those who say: "There was a time when He was not," and "Before being begotten He was not," or who declare that He was made from nothing, or that the Son of God is from a different substance or being, or subject to change and alteration, such persons the Catholic and apostolic Church condemns.

SYMBOL OF THE FIRST GENERAL COUNCIL OF CONSTANTINOPLE
(AD 381)

We believe in one God, the Father almighty, maker of heaven and earth, of all things visible and invisible. And in one Lord Jesus Christ, the only-begotten Son of God, generated from the Father before all ages, Light from Light, true God from true God, begotten, not made, one in being with the Father, through whom all things were made. For us men and for our salvation He came down from the heavens, and became flesh from the Holy Spirit and the Virgin Mary and was made man. For our sake too He was crucified under Pontius Pilate, suffered and was buried. On the third day He rose again according to the Scriptures, He ascended to the heavens and is seated at the right hand of the Father. He shall come again in glory to judge the living and the dead; to His Kingdom there will be no end.

And in the Holy Spirit, the Lord and Giver of life, who proceeds from the Father, who together with the Father and the Son is worshipped and glorified, who has spoken through the prophets. (And) in one Holy Catholic and apostolic Church. We acknowledge one baptism for the forgiveness of sins. We expect the resurrection of the dead and the life of the world to come. Amen.

THE SYMBOL OF ST AMBROSE OF MILAN
(Pre AD 397)

I believe in God, the Father almighty, and in Jesus Christ, His only Son, our Lord, who was born of the Virgin Mary by the Holy Spirit, who suffered under Pontius Pilate, died and was buried. On the third day He rose again from the dead. He ascended into heaven, and is seated at the right hand of the Father, wherefrom He shall come to judge the living and the dead. And in the Holy Spirit, the Holy Church, the forgiveness of sins and the resurrection of the body.

THE SYMBOL OF ST RUFINUS OF AQUILAEA
(c. AD 404)

I believe in God, the Father almighty, invisible and impassible, and in Jesus Christ, His only Son, our Lord, who was born of the Virgin Mary by the Holy Spirit, was crucified under Pontius Pilate and was buried. He went down to the dead. On the third day He rose again from the dead. He ascended into heaven, and is seated at the right hand of the Father. From there He shall come to judge the living and the dead. And in the Holy Spirit, the Holy Church, the forgiveness of sins and the resurrection of the body.

THE 'FAITH OF DAMASUS'
(5th CENTURY)

We believe in one God, the Father almighty, and in our one Lord Jesus Christ, the Son of God, and in [one] Holy Spirit, God. We do not worship and confess three Gods, but one God who is Father and Son and Holy Spirit. He is one God, yet not solitary; He is not at the same time Father to Himself and Son, but the Father is He who begets and the Son He who is begotten. As for the Holy Spirit, He is neither begotten nor unbegotten (ingenious), neither created nor made, but He proceeds from the Father and the Son, being equally eternal and fully equal with the Father and the Son and cooperating with them; for it is written: "By the Word of the Lord the heavens were made," that is, by the Son of God, "and all their host by the breath of His mouth;" and elsewhere: "When you send forth your Spirit, they are created, and you renew the face of the earth." Therefore, in the name of the Father and of the Son and of the Holy Spirit we confess one God, for the term 'God' refers to power, not to personal characteristics. The proper name for the Father is Father, and the proper name for the Son is Son, and the proper name for the Holy Spirit is Holy

Spirit. And in this Trinity we believe that God (is) one because what is of one nature and of one substance and of one power with the Father is from one Father. The Father begets the Son, not by an act of will, nor out of necessity, but by nature. In the last times, the Son, who never ceased to be with the Father, came down from the Father to save us and to fulfil the Scriptures. He was conceived from the Holy Spirit and born of the Virgin Mary. He assumed body, soul and sensibility, that is, a complete human nature. He did not lose what He was, but began to be what He was not, in such a way, however, that He is perfect in His own nature and truly shares in ours. For, He who was God has been born as a man, and He who has been born as a man acts as God; and He who acts as God dies as man, and He who dies as man rises again as God. Having conquered the power of death with that body with which He had been born and had suffered and died, He rose again on the third day; He ascended to the Father and is seated at His right hand in the glory which He always has had and always has. We believe that we who have been cleansed in His death and in His blood shall be raised up by Him on the last day in this body in which we now live. It is our hope that we shall receive from Him eternal life, the reward of good merit, or else (we shall receive) the penalty of eternal punishment for sins. Read these words, keep them, subject your soul to this faith. From Christ the Lord you will receive both life and reward.

THE PSEUDO-ATHANASIAN SYMBOL 'QUICUMQUE' (END OF THE 5th CENTURY)

Whoever wishes to be saved must, first of all, hold the Catholic faith, for, unless he keeps it whole and inviolate, he will undoubtedly perish for ever. Now this is the Catholic faith: We worship one God in the Trinity and the Trinity in unity, without either confusing the persons or dividing the substance; for the person of the Father is one, the Son's is another, the Holy Spirit's another; but the Godhead of Father, Son and Holy Spirit is one, their glory equal, their majesty equally eternal. Such as the Father is, such is the Son, such also the Holy Spirit; uncreated is the Father, uncreated the Son, uncreated the Holy Spirit; infinite is the Father, infinite the Son, infinite the Holy Spirit; eternal is the Father, eternal the Son, eternal the Holy Spirit; yet, they are not three eternal beings but one eternal, just as they are not three uncreated beings or three infinite beings but one uncreated and one infinite. In the same way, almighty is the Father, almighty the Son, almighty the Holy Spirit; yet, they are not three almighty beings but one almighty. Thus, the Father is God, the Son is God, the Holy Spirit is God; yet, they are not three gods but one God. Thus, the Father is Lord, the Son is Lord, the Holy Spirit is Lord; yet, they are not three lords but one Lord. For, as the Christian truth compels us to acknowledge each person distinctly as God and Lord, so too the Catholic religion forbids us to speak of three gods or lords. The Father has neither been made by anyone, nor is He created or begotten; the Son is from the Father alone, not made nor created but begotten; the Holy Spirit is from the Father and the Son, not made nor created nor begotten, but proceeding. So there is one Father, not three Fathers; one Son, not three Sons; one Holy Spirit, not three Holy Spirits. And in this Trinity there is no before or after, no greater or lesser, but all three persons are equally eternal with each other and fully equal. Thus, in all things, as has already been stated above, both unity in the Trinity and Trinity in the unity must be worshipped. Let him therefore who wishes to be saved think this of the Trinity. For his eternal salvation it is necessary, however that he should also faithfully believe in the incarnation of our Lord Jesus Christ. Here then is the right faith: We believe and confess that our Lord Jesus Christ, the Son of God, is both and equally God and man. He is God from the substance of the Father, begotten before the ages, and He is man from the substance of a mother, born in time; perfect God and perfect man, composed of a rational soul and a human body; equal to the Father as to His divinity, less than the Father as to His humanity. Although He is God and man, He is nevertheless one Christ, not two; however, not one because the divinity has been changed into a human body, but because the humanity has been assumed into God; entirely one, not by a confusion of substance but by the unity of personhood. For, as a rational soul and a body are a single man, so God and man are one Christ. He suffered for our salvation, went down to the underworld, rose again from the dead on the third day, ascended to the heavens, is seated at the right hand of the Father, wherefrom He shall come to judge the living and the dead. At His coming all men are to rise again with their bodies and to render an account of their own deeds; those who have done good will go to eternal life, but those who have done evil to eternal fire. This is the Catholic faith. Unless one believes it faithfully and firmly, he cannot be saved.

Acknowledgments

Scripture quotes extracted from the *Revised Standard Version of the Bible* (Catholic Edition), copyright © 1946, 1952 and 1971.

The Catholic Encyclopaedia (1911).

Anne W. Carroll, *Christ the King: Lord of History*, 2nd Ed., Trinity Communications, 1986.

Warren H. Carroll, *The Founding of Christendom* (A History of Christendom), Vol. 1, Christendom Press, 1985.

Eusebius, *The History of the Church*, Penguin Classics, 1989.

F. X. Funk, *A Manual of Church History*, Vol. 1, Burns Oates & Washbourne, 1931.

Michael Grant, *History of Rome*, Book Club Associates, 1978, pp. 321-331.

Fernard Hayward, *A History of the Popes*, J.M. Dent & Sons Ltd., 1931.

Philip Hughes, *A History of the Church*, Vol. 1, Sheed and Ward, 1948.

Rev. William A. Jurgens, *The Faith of the Early Fathers*, Copyright © 1970 by The Order of St Benedict, Inc. Published by The Liturgical Press, Collegeville, Minnesota.

Josephus, *The Jewish War*, Penguin Classics, 1959.

Fr John Laux, *Church History*, TAN Books and Publishers, 1930.

Andrew Louth, *Early Christian Writers*, Penguin Books, 1968.

Rev. D. I. Lanslots, *The Primitive Church*, TAN Books and Publishers, 1926.

Rev. L. G. Lovasik, *The Catholic Church through the Ages*, Catholic Book Publishing Co., 1990.

Denis Meadows, *A Short History of the Catholic Church*, Robert Hale Ltd., 1959.

Abbot Giuseppe Ricciotti, *The Age of Martyrs – Christianity from Diocletian to Constantine*, TAN Books and Publishers, 1959.

James Stevenson, *The Catacombs – Life and Death in Early Christianity*, Thomas Nelson Publishers, 1978.

Tixeront – Raemers, A *Handbook of Patrology*, B. Herder Book Co., 1946.

About the Author

Robert M. Haddad holds qualifications in law, theology, philosophy and religious education, namely, a LL.B (USyd.), Grad. Cert. in RE (Charles Sturt Uni.), Grad. Dip. Ed. (ACU), Grad. Dip. in Teacher Ed. (College of Teachers, London), AMLP (Oxon.), MA Theo. Studies (UNDA – University Medalist), MRelEd (UNDA) and a M. Phil (ACU). For his M. Phil. Robert researched the apologetical arguments of St Justin Martyr.

In addition to his studies, Robert has also authored various books, including *Lord of History Series* (2 volumes), *Law and Life*, *The Family and Human Life*, *Defend the Faith!*, *The Case for Christianity – St Justin Martyr's Arguments for Religious Liberty and Judicial Justice*, *Answering the Anti-Catholic Challenge* (ch. 3) and *1001 Reasons Why it's Great to be Catholic!*

From 1990-2005, Robert worked full-time at St Charbel's College, Sydney, teaching Religion and History. He held the positions of Year Co-ordinator and Religious Education Co-ordinator concurrently for ten years and was Assistant Principal (Welfare) for six years.

From 2006-2008, Robert worked full-time as the Convener of the Catholic Chaplaincy at the University of Sydney. He was also a lecturer at the Center for Thomistic Studies for eleven years (1996-2008), teaching Apologetics, Church Fathers and Church History, as well as assisting part-time with *Lumen Verum Apologetics* (1996-present) and the Catholic Adult Education Centre (2010-2013).

From 2009-2012, Robert was the Director of the Confraternity of Christian Doctrine (Sydney) and in that capacity was the chief editor of the revised *Christ our Light and Life* (3rd Edition) religious education K-12 curriculum used by Catholic students in state schools as well as the *Gratia Series* sacramental programs for children preparing for Reconciliation, First Holy Communion, and Confirmation in the Archdiocese of Sydney. He has recently also edited a new RCIA resource for use in Catholic schools in the same Archdiocese entitled *Initiate*.

In 2014, Robert was awarded an Australia Day Award by the Australia Day Council of New South Wales for his overall contribution to education. Currently, he is the Head of New Evangelization for the Catholic Education Office (Sydney) and lectures/tutors in Theology at the University of Notre Dame, Sydney. From time to time Robert also appears on the Telepace Television Network and Voice of Charity radio.

Other Works by the Author

Introduction to the Greatest Fathers of the Church (Parousia Media, 1999)

A Seat at the Supper (General Editor; author Frank Colyer, self-published, 2001)

The Apostles' Creed (Parousia Media, 2004)

Law and Life (Parousia Media, 2004)

The Case for Christianity – St Justin Martyr's Arguments for Religious Liberty and Judicial Justice (Connor Court Publishing, 2009)

The Family and Human Life (2nd Ed. co-authored with Bernard Toutounji, Parousia Media, 2011)

Defend the Faith! (Parousia Media, 2012)

Answering the Anti-Catholic Challenge (General Editor and author of ch. 3, Modotti Press, 2012)

1001 Reasons Why it's Great to be Catholic! (Parousia Media, 2014)

Christ our Light and Life (General Editor 3rd Edition, 2012) religious education curriculum K-12 used by Catholic students in government schools throughout the state of New South Wales.

Gratia Series (General Editor, 2012) sacramental programs for children preparing for Reconciliation, First Holy Communion, and Confirmation in the Archdiocese of Sydney.

Initiate (General Editor, CEO Sydney Publications, 2014), a RCIA resource for use in Catholic schools in the Archdiocese of Sydney.

www.ingramcontent.com/pod-product-compliance
Lightning Source LLC
Chambersburg PA
CBHW071626080526
44588CB00010B/1287